AUTHOR
IN SEARCH OF
SIX CHARACTERS

JOEL ROSENBLUM

iUniverse, Inc.
Bloomington

Author In Search Of Six Characters

iUniverse books may be ordered through booksellers or by contacting:

iUniverse
1663 Liberty Drive
Bloomington, IN 47403
www.iuniverse.com
1-800-Authors (1-800-288-4677)

ISBN: 978-1-4620-7192-0 (sc)
ISBN: 978-1-4620-7193-7 (e)

Printed in the United States of America

iUniverse rev. date: 01/12/2012

a (very) forward

FOREWARD

by Grim Reader

What could be more improbable than an author who joins his own characters in the story he is writing?

It's as if he comes from a land where nobody suits him anymore. He craves literary revenge against a world full of unsympathetic publishers and out-of-order readers, and he takes on the prospect of melding himself from the reality of creative thought into his own fiction. He seems to think the perfect novel is one in which he can just go away and live in.

The present crowds around him. Eventually, he escapes to search for and join in with his characters. Their fabricated existence can rehabilitate him. They may even reject him but what an adventure! His projected personification might be that of a runaway or, as he calls himself, a *fugitive*. And soon, off he goes, predestined to give up his authority over them in order to enliven the mix of his people. All the more appealing in this adventure is the unexpected freedom for his six players-on-the-page unaware, it would seem, that it is N present in their company.

Indeed, the writer of this book calls himself "N" and, if I ask for more, I am only left to assume this is the covert form for his role as Narrator and the beginning of more cryptic matters to come.

As painters in classical times would often picture themselves in their works to symbolize their being a witness and just as a playwright will join his cast on the theater stage in a desire to share their dramatics, N has that same fancy. (We learn that there was many a frivolous impulse when N attended the theater, that he yearned to go up on the stage and join the gathering of players in their conversation so he could be in company with such interesting people. He frequented all the dramas of Chekhov, Ibsen, Strindberg, etc.)

Every writer of fiction is a schizophrene anyway. And as he disappears into his work, he figuratively martyrs himself for his art. N's razzle-dazzle concept understandably whets him to expect some bizarre moments of illumination.

I had this brief conversation with him.

GR   Where shall we start? You begin writing kind of a mystery memoir. Eventually, you withdraw from the narrative part of the story line so you can join the characters in your own little thriller. You fictionalize yourself. Certainly a baroque style of writing. What do you call it?

N   I call it 'fugitive literature.'

GR   An escape from real life by establishing your presence in a fictitious one. What is it you are seeking to get away from?

N   *All art is escapism, isn't it? Here. Let me read you a letter I recently wrote to all publishers. It goes, "Dear Publishers: This time I am not in any way petitioning for acceptance of my writing as I won't be sending it to you. Therefore, this will dismiss all those sporadic forebodings in the depths of my heart, no further interest in even getting my stuff read and no more odious rejections from you. Yes, dear nitpickers: I am now forever free from being scrutinized, criticized, pigeon-holed, tortured and starved. It will no longer mean being committed to some fragile psychological state...down there somewhere, shut in, alone with my soul. No! You petty printers can go on believing that all writers have their bouts of insanity just for your amusement and profit. But not this one. Be advised that for me the caprices of patronage are moonish now. Sincerely yours."*

GR   *Sounds like rather a routine rant at the publishing community.*

N   *That merciless pack of exalted humiliation. I die no more for them.*

GR   *The end of literary torment, then? No more dreaming on paper.*

N   *Well put.*

GR   *Of course, no more readers either. Complete nullity for a writer, wouldn't you think?*

N What do writers want from readers anyway? An author is first demeaned by publishers. Then perennially mocked by a bunch of once-over rummagers who only read fiction to get to the next page. I am weary of writing, reading, editing, day-dreaming, starting over, To seek publication is to be damned. It's time for me to recover from the angst of authorship.

GR While you simultaneously prepare for the next passage. The story of the six characters.

N Yes, it is that story! "Author In Search Of Six Characters." To seek out the six. Everything positively printed out in my head. All I have to do is let the inhabitants arrange the words.

GR Considering the title of your work, you seem to be simulating or, shall I say, turning upside down the Pirandello play, "Six Characters In Search Of An Author."

N Somewhat. But I'm just the opposite of Pirandello. His creatures are in comic agony. They realize they were born as characters in an unfinished play. Their fictional lives are being denied further dramatic action. Halted in time without resolution, without peace. They have been living a story and then the drama of it all has broken down. Their fictional lives *need further portrayal. They need completion; they're searching for an author to finish their tale. That's the deal on his people, so very desperate to chance upon a writer. Whereas, my somebodies require no part of an author. It is I searching for them. Not the other way around. I want to join them, as they live beyond my rehearsals. Yes, I have designed personalities but they are creating their own possibilities now, continuing to live their stories. And, I can tell you, once on the page, these players may be bent on controlling their creator .*

GR   Controlling a god is a lot of work. What kind of characters are they?

N   A strange gallery of six. Let's see: an heiress, a professional comedian, his passed-up ex, a priest, a jazz musician and a woman of pleasure. And they are all beautifully moon-struck.

And that's all I got out of N. With this conversation, I left him sitting outdoors in a special state of consciousness and a mind fired up with the intrigue of disappearance.

So, a forward march to the workings of an author who declares himself not intended for publication. Beginning with the title, there is obviously everything about writer N's kind of literary spree that evokes the extraordinary creations in the 1921 stage play

"Six Characters In Search Of An Author" by Luigi Pirandello.

Both of these odd existentialists have conceived inhabitants and then have abandoned their authority, quoting P: "Creatures of my spirit, these six phantoms of art are lost without an author as now I am lost without them." N, however, is saying, "These individuals are living a life which is now their own and not mine anymore, a life which is not in my power to deny them. So, we shall all get together and have them entertain me." He would join in their circle as a sort of mystery crasher.

Now it is N in post-Pirandello mode: a vanishing novelist intent on writing his way out of his memoirs and into some essence beyond existence. "There is no plot," says N of his novel. It's about his desire then. His romantic risks take him "to search them out and join their drama."

His published life has not been entirely ignominious. He has in print a flight of short pieces. Titles and story lines are all extremely sardonic.

"YOU DON'T WANT TO BE ME" - suddenly, whenever it's activated, a pull-string doll begins spouting advice and comments on scientific and philosophical matters

"THAT WAS YESTERDAY" - pedophilia having become a raging international crisis, children have begun assassinating priests. The Pope is in mortal danger!

"SCATTERED CRAYONS" - a number of women are mysteriously called together as they soon discover all had an affair with the same man.

"NOTE" - the stuck horn of an empty delivery truck in a desolate field blows its constant, solitary sound. Each day, ambitious players arrive, unpack their various instruments and riff along, improvising to the single tone. One day, a bird……

"NOW SHOWING" - a serial playwright abducts 6 people and seals each one in a separate room of his deserted motel…he plans to force them to learn the dialogue of an original drama and promises their release as soon as they perform the play with himself in the role of a mystery guest.

POETRY SAMPLES N E X T

N's vague attempts at poetry were often just epigrams, such as:

…poetry has two inspirations - sadness or fun

…if only people could be more like books…in that they would give the information we want to know without the information that will make us feel bad

Or full-blown rhymes:

no questions asked
none taken
say we've basked
in pools of Jamaican
willingly unmasked

Or puns:

I have weather angst
wary of hurricangst
hip hip hooray though
if there's no tornado

Or the Almighty:

as God has rejected my early removal
rhyming's become quite the mind's catalyst
when all I want is a stamp of approval
with Himself the Eternal, Philatelist

In AISO6, N rails against his tormentors and evokes that strange disorder of the mind that "those filthy publishers revel in" but none of whom will be reading him. He wants them all tripping over each other's professional stagnation. For N now, any publication irremediably cheapens and falsifies his viewpoint. Does this author know he's not supposed to get too sensitive in this line of work?

N's real life turns into fiction and his fictional life becomes real, designed as a vehicle for venturing into a world turned over to the inmates six. Do his characters truly have free choice? N likes to think so and even gives up his authority in order to join them.

I do come to praise, not to bury him. There's lots of time to a muse.

Forget Pirandello...N is now getting around to telling his story.

AUTHOR IN SEARCH OF SIX CHARACTERS

I

Today's outdoors is working well. The trees help me. Not the old ones so much but those that I planted grow thickly in the wind of trust. A sudden breeze picks up. Palm happenings amid the afternoon slices of light as streaked across the lawn in newly-minted shades of green. My dry sherry floats its few fragments of ice. Like that of any drinker, my consciousness is continuously being towed to a better place.

Writers need the power of landscape. Consider that trees turn into books. Hurrah for nature's inspiration and, for me especially, my deliverance from unpublished torment. The tropical alfresco free my mind. Where I am sitting at this moment, the day's beauty overtouches all potentials and possibilities of literary rejection. I have, indeed, declared my freedom in a letter disassociating myself from any publishers. I am no longer a writer in bondage. I can let my ego flow from imagination to ink without a thought of myself—in print or out. Wonderful feeling. Because I am fed up with a seat somewhere in biblio-Siberia. No editor will I need. My life will nevermore be challenged by critics on salaries. No new marriages for me to the media. No more best-seller woes. No showbiz fights, no celebrity tours; gone the lonely task of writing for riches and fame. Gone also, sadly of course, is the drip of royalty dollars, fluid………gracious……… monotonous………

But yes! Fie to the brutalities of pop culture's demands…the caprices of patronage. No more stranded on the editor's iceberg, stabbed with pens and so desperate to hear the two words never to come: "Film Rights." Goodbye! disapproval and rejection. Farewell! notoriety. Addio! houses of print, stores of manuscripts never even read. Free frees of all that stifles a writer: publisher cruelty, absent muse and bored gods! Gone all commercial armor. No waiting for that phone call…printing house, agent, publicist, reporter or feckless well-wisher. Enough in company with those scribblers, styled as dramatists in the scene and herd, nothing more than ventriloquists saying over and over again, "I suffer; therefore, I am."

To be or not allowed to be. I am a portrait...a moment in time, a person alone now in a lighter, more graceful world . Only a single preface-writer makes his forward strides with me. I write write write but forever more only in the wind. My journals are loosed, sloosed, unleashed, splashed. *They do not have to make sense if the indifference to them equally makes no sense>* aha.

Meantime, life itself becomes its own fiction occurring even at this moment as I repose outdoors, drink, write, discover the soul, maintain some luxurious indolence in the lucid air and companioned by the CD's of classical and jazz maestros. The endless optimism of a bounding tropical nature...bestowing its breeze, its greenery, the enchantments of distance and even an occasional eagerness of raindrops to distill the mind. Only now, a blessed combination of Mahler, tropical warmth and dry sherry dreams me along in sunlight and sounds.

I'm just one of nature's experiments
what will I plan today
that I can lie about tomorrow

Once, when I sat here in the backyard absent my muse who was hiding off as usual in the trees of someone else's orchard, I wanted just to understand Einstein. And failed. It is: mass in motion varies in space and time. So nothing in the universe is at rest except in relation to something else? Is that enough to get into? When I stand up, I can't even understand the presence of the breeze - how the same, mild, wafting wind-force can be so gentle and serene upon my face while simultaneously applying that same casual power to incite the great branches of the stalwart trees.

At least, Einstein draws the mind up to the liberating effect of space where the universe has existed forever without explanation of why it exists. Eternity utters its day like a perfume over every surrounding surface. The self becomes someone else.

The perfect novel is one you can live in. Self-invention and self-deceit. Each writer haunts his own story and so: what if he were to assume a presence among some formerly created personations? Those strange place-settings of my last imaginings that are called "characters" would be face-to-face with their author. Suppose the creatures of my spirit—former phantoms of art—have gone on, already living a life which is their own and not mine any more, an existence which is beyond my power to deny them. Luigi Pirandello staged the echo version of this notion in his "Six Characters In Search Of An Author" and called it Mirror Theater. Why shouldn't I try this out? After all, up till now, it is only me *not* doing it.

It would be to exit this graveyard of literary theories and become a fictional character in my own novel! Is it so awful to be looking for people I can set store in? Madness explaining itself. The vagabond author escapes the scrutiny of others - a bit of worldly martyrdom of spirit or outrage or, God forbid, exploring a talent.

And what scarifying delights await! There will be something spiteful among "my" six, a percolating sense of new independence from their previous god...especially intimidating, considering the expectations with which I will become incidental to and no longer responsible for the life and drama of my creations. After all, what I—for the most part—want for myself is professional fulfillment, the world's love and respect, sexual passion forever renewable, peace of mind, an occasional, unattended piano and supernatural reassurance.

For this, all I need to do is to become a mental choreographer to organize my persona from genesis to exodus, from creation to escape.

II

Owning the air just now...this moment soaked with sexual floatations...be-wilderment... chronic new involvement...musical addiction... sockless statements...cocktail sherry...intelligent hedonism...libretto matched to bird-calls...time, the only critic...happy days seasoned with spirits. Oh, see the brief, little ant moving along the page I'm writing on, going his way across as a current of air suddenly summons him!

(maybe give the wine and the moment a little poetry, yes?)

> was today so successful
> that the tiniest of bugs crawling across my writing pad
> is silently examined rather than made to be stressful
> insect, begone! away to another god! while I am here still
> writing mad

The same wind suddenly rushes across me, lifting away my printed, reading material. I accidentally tip my glass as I snatch at the pages. Must restore my attention. Things now tidy, I grab up a fallen ice cube and throw it to the darkness beneath the philodendren and, as it melts, wonder at a lizard's possible discovery.

> *ink in pen*
> *impoverished pad*
> *write again*
> *the life you've had*

Miracles always impose conditions: a bird looks about and begins to sing, for example. I listen a few times and then provide a line of lyrics to fit the quick tune they all try to sell. Birds once represented souls as they could surely fly up to heaven. Artists drew them with such obsessive accuracy because they were symbols of freedom. Way back then, few creatures could change their positions very much. Only dreamers and the birds. An outspread wing on a thermal current to overcome the wrench of gravity as the flight bequeaths nothing but a wonderment. What's intriguing is the unseen calculation of exact up-versus-down balance, of the miraculous against memory. Brushstrokes in the air. Nature joined to art.

I am a mirage
everybody else
gets to suppose me
I am an oasis
a horizon
an empty parking space
somewhere

The architect Gaudi declared, "My teachers are the trees." Gaudi's ardent imagination flew off to distant horizons, the same as when a writer's perfect-eureka creative thought floats to the surface. Synaptic miracle. Nature should be the language of *architexture*. Stand in the forest. Look up and find the domes, arches and prayer spaces that rise to God and His angels in heaven. From music we learn how to move (dance); from architecture, we learn how to protect (sanctuary).

Architecture, the only art that requires travel. I like the haunted silence of this creative discipline. And it's the only one that must be perfect. Or else things fall down. Ask the co-conspirators—the engineers—who have to get their identity by designing architecture into giant structural expressionism.

Just as nature distributes its whims, the architect fills up his spaces, and the writers sort through their memories. I am always fascinated when I read what architects write. Not the jargon and minutiae of their profession but rather opinions and concerns beyond their professional activities. A comment in an architectural essay I chanced to read was so delectable for my story-telling soul. It was:

"From a single, catastrophic moment, a space emerges made only of light. This space undergoes unforeseen changes, and soon we are well beyond the sanctuary of order and reason." Thus, the writer-designer reveals a dialogue between the structuring of architecture (space) and the formation of images into sentences (exposition).

As they relate to the spirit of architectural authorship, a few, scattered, blueprint bromides follow:

elements in tension:
beam. arch, suspension, cable, clouds, forest, earth, the open

a building, unlike a novel, cannot simply be put away...a sentinel mocking the past

a cloud is a bundle of turnings...the horizon belongs neither to the heavens nor the earth

III

It's a breather to quote other writers. One has an extreme and unique relation in reading and sometimes just excerpting somebody's prose. Yes, it is boring and depressing not always being creative enough to make your own statements. A writer's life is one long bout of plagiarism and spelling horrors.

"plagiarize!
don't let a single thing evade your eyes!"
...tom lehrer

I steal from every every single detail ever thought, ever scribbled down on paper, ever published, ever noted on a blank score. I have appropriated everything I can, every word, every phrase, every paragraph, every idea, sentiment, quotation, epiphany and song. Neither poetry nor fashion has eluded my portraiture. No thirties or forties film. Not a note of syncopation or riff of improvisation has eluded my "creative" grasp. Not a whiff of Wilde or Woolf has been lost to my pen. If all humankind were to cease its creativity, I could only provide the blank page, the empty stage and the ego's rage. If my work has anything, it is that I am taking this from this and that from that and mixing them together. If people don't approve of it, they can be brilliant their own way. I steal from all great artists. They don't need homage, especially from me. They're all just there for me to say to them, as Cagney once pulled out his gat and snarled, "I'm after you now, you dirty, yellow-bellied rat! Come out and give it up or I'll blast you right through the door!"

I am the resurrection of imitation in all categories. Some merely have wishful thinking about this practice. Shakespeare appropriated like crazy. So did T.S. Eliot. But if these guys are examples of plagiarism, then we want more thieves. The copier has added value to the original. Why interrupt a fast-paced narrative to confess something bound by quotation marks when a predecessor of mine has said what I want to say better than I can! Readers are not professional arbiters, and most don't care a straw about literary vandalism. The public wants a good read, a good show or a good, round-the-campfire spooker. In my justification, I do not counterfeit out of sheer laziness or forgetfulness, the latter being the standard defense. After all, reading is just thinking with someones else brain. Here's to the writer whose offering glitters with stolen gold!

The only honorable form of usurping the work of others is by letting their music flow into me, nourishing the imagination when I'm writing. Listening to music while acting the writer is primal and, by nature, asocial. Concentration puts you at a remove, and solitude is inevitable. No one speaks. You are alone. The very air owns you.

While doing the work of the pirate, why be jealously conerned about the words of others? Better to waste your occasional lack of talent by coveting an art form you cannot possibly steal from: professional acting, say. I'm looking at a photograph of Orson Welles in his thirties. God. Just to see his handsome presence is to hear the voice of bottled thunder so deeply engaged in worldly pronouncements. Oh, to take the measure of that unique resonance and polished presence! I would see his theatrical self as a million times my own pretensions. But it is still that of a million times SOMETHING, not a million times ZERO. The damnable abomination of other people's talent!

The motion picture - turning paper into celluloid.

Movies are just art showing you the way people should look. Most actresses read their first scripts to find out what clothes they're going to wear. In addition, their historical, Hollywood heroes must have mystery. That is, unless certain people get in front of the cameras because they can dance. These ones don't have to act.

Fred and Ginger moved to the music for years without stopping even to be properly introduced or without altering the photography-ready smile Fred acquired dancing so many years with his sister. Where is this man now we need him with his total disregard of the hardship and despair of today to show that art need have nothing to do with life. That's where *Citizen Kane* exposes itself so heavy-handedly about America. Although, Charles Foster 'Welles' did dance with the chorus girls he brought to his party...alas, the big man left us all forever looking for that Rosebud. Who would want to dare beyond the burning sled of lost youth?

Brando's another one - a slumming Stanislavski, dedicated to making vulnerability irresistable. A brutish Don Juan. Why do the great ones so rarely have the talent to handle their genius - Orson Welles on the path of brilliant promise - Jackson Pollock's art of chaos. Charlie Parker's flights of jazz dreaming him into heroin addiction. I shall disappear into my art as they did. What is talent anyway, said Noel Coward, except instinct plus taste?

What makes us artistic anyway? Must one be a neurotic to be creative? Is there some sinister legend holding that without mental illness, the creative spark will die? Do the clever ones have to refuse therapy out of a fear that, in losing compulsions and obsessions, they will also decrease not only their prized individuality but also their zeal and their touch? They might want rid of their manic miseries but they still do not want the process of getting well to make them different from whatever they were before. Are they thinking that their habits of madness will ease their torments and make their artistic work possible? Nietzsche's lifelong malady and his resistance against it raised mental illness to the rank of metaphysical order. Dostoevsky looked upon illness as a profound source of wisdom. Van Gogh did not paint his way out of an asylum, however.

To link genius with insanity is an unhappy luxury. Humans hate the concept of the need for permutation of any kind; yet, the aptitude for change is an unmistakable sign of mental health. The essence of psychical illness is the freezing of behavior into unalterable and insatiable patterns. There seems to be a strange and defensive fear that giving up one's neuroses willl destroy creativity. Being a neurotic person is like a novel in that neither he nor it has a future.

INSANITY IS THE RIGIDITY OF SYSTEM.

Ah! the burden of awareness.

Most of us go to our graves with our music still inside us. Mine is in Sisyphean residence and continuously splashes about my mind to pour out rashly at the sight of any keyboard.

The beginning musician who doesn't read music plays by ear; so the only way to teach her is by rote. Volunteering as I did one time to bring piano to kindergarteners, and with no clue where to take them musically, I got each one of 16 tykes pounding away at "Chopsticks." And. As they counted with me out loud ONE two three, ONE two three, ONE two three, I myself began to realize the miracle of their subliminally storing away the splendid essence of time in music and, indeed, in life. The heartbeat is timing. Breathing is rhythmic. Clocks tick in time. Music is sound through time. Everywhere there exists the measured tempo of beats and expectations.

Is there a psychological similarity between tuneful training and abuse? Are many young children psychically beaten to musical suffering, pushed onto a piano bench, deprived of thoughts of recess, stripped of their playthings, even the abstract toys of their dreamy fantasies; and then, even throughout the torment (never pleasure), their uncooperative talent will not devise the slightest philosophical reward, their little artistic, inner angst enforcing its war against peace of mind. Knowledge which is acquired under compulsion has no hold on the intellect.

So many sight-readers marvel at the jazz pianist improvising through any standard tune picking up and laying down *extempore* on something merely hummed at him and forever resident in a musician's sensitive belief that everything will be OK today if we could all sit down together at a universal jam session. Jazz is the sound of autobiography. Even for those who can't read music and can't sing on key either, it is still amazing how the mind remembers so much music. This is all part of God's plan because music gives Him a lot of time to rest. (except when it's hymns.)

For astrologists, the melodies of the spheres is the voice of destiny. All the planets orbit and vibrate in perfect musical harmony inevitably producing celestial "music." The Greeks loved music but it could not be written down; singers had to memorize 80 hours of song, all of Beethoven and Mozart. The music business has always been a cruel and shallow money trench where thieves and pimps run loose, and good men die like dogs. There is also a negative side.

Countless composers inspire the poet. I am almost always struck to tears when immersed in something symphonic, dramatic and emotional as Schubert or Mendelssohn in that many human beings with their chosen instruments and their talents are expressing themselves together—in perfection—and the entire purpose of their ideal is infallibly following notes on a page dedicated by genius. An orchestra represents an ideal society. People working together for excellence, and everybody else gets to sit still and shut up as it is an occasion to consider the colossal experiences of the composer.

MUSIC MU$IC MU$I$ That looks dangerous enough. Music remembers. Words, though. Words convince. If only they would bandage the heart a little more. But turning melody into literature! One composes to populate the world with ghosts. One writes to create lives.

Oh, if I could produce a melodic masterwork that would march us all away to battle, I would completely give up thoughts of authorship.

IV

While at one of several colleges, I took up writing fiction to the sound of classics and discovered "Rite of Spring" to be absolutely empowering. Stravinski's extravagance drove my imagination to create a story beginning on a mysterious train-ride with no place to stop. Everytime I summon "Rite…." soon comes the steady, haunting, beating impression of a moving train. Take it from there!

MAHLER. Thinking about Gustav Mahler. His intoxicating, Fifth Symphony Adagietto is playing for me now. Like my Stravinski railroad car, this passage of Mahler's doesn't want to end, and if it ends, I have forgotten that time has passed. Just digging Mahler but not trying to understand him, he's saying, "I'm insane, don't listen to me." I like Mahler's romantic ideas and dynamic bombast. I especially like that he seems to know my emotional interest. This leads to oneness for composer and for writer.

Someone in a recent movie said, "Wouldn't you just *die* without Mahler?"

Gustav Mahler could never get a complete opera to the the publishing house and neither will I undertake to be paid for appearing in print, my previous short stories published in mute testimony that only the very modest of my work escaped dismissal. But the on-coming *dramatis personnae* are gathered from, plucked out of these little tales, and soon I will be the fugitive departing the mind's theater and allowing those in the blend to design their own drama and myself to join them wherever they are now. In this yarn of Six Characters, I intend to co-act in their intrigue. My own evanescence beckons me to the company of the very souls I have created.

But Mahler: his Jewish background made him a target for Vienna's racist newspapers even beyond his decision to convert. How anomalous it was that this symphonist found inspiration in Richard Wagner's rich, romantic pictures in sound. Mahler the persecuted Jew and Wagner the revolting, bigoted, racist megalomaniac. There's nothing to gasp about here. It was in Wagner's writings and not just his operas that Nazi propagandists found his pseudo-intellectual claptrap serving to underpin their crude utterings. More than Wagner's celebration of Germanic heroes like Sigfried and Tannhauser, there was present an ugly, racist undertone that was to have a powerful and predictable effect on the Nazis. Of course, Wagner's music can be and has been separated from the poison that spewed from his venomous pen. There is no denying the ambition and musical importance of this composer's work—its great power and great passion cannot be denied. Pity it is that he was so under-endowed in humaneness.

Anti-Semitism is a concept of a prosperous minority destined for constant scorn, represnting an inherited aberration of the non-Jewish human mind seeking a way to blame an entire people when things go wrong. Judeophobes represent piety united in a chosen myth that Jews are responsible for the crucifixion. Even more virile is Arab bigotry, political and mobilized to eliminate Judaism. The irony beyond it all is the chosen myth that Jews control industry, the media and academia. This beautiful lie must answer to this: how then have the other two Abrahamic religions endured so thoroughly under such a Judaic cultural hegemony? Meantime, there is no great, intellectual movement in which the Jews do not greatly participate and invigorate.

Even Christian fundamentalists who regard Jews as descendants of Christ preach that the estabishment of the state of Israel is a prelude to the conversion of the Hebrews to be followed happily enough by Armageddon and the consigning of the non-converts to hell. Another irony lurks in that if they had actually successfully proselityzed all Jews, the Christians would have no one to leave behind on That Last Great Day. Nevertheless, if there is to be a Judgment Day, the Almighty's Promised Land for the Jews won't be Israel; it will be, as it is now, the abiding home for many wanderers and victims: America.

Meanwhile, every day, Muslims are killed by Muslims. Too few are the Islamic leaders who see fit to get up and say enough is enough. It's a world where if Christians kill Muslims, it's a crusade. If Jews kill Muslims, it's a massacre. And when Muslims kill Muslims, its the weather channel. The silence of Islam makes Allah weep!

Poor God, through all this. I miss Him back when he was inspiring Italian painting and French stained glass, German music and English chapter houses, Russian ballet and Latin rhythms and when the consumption of culture was sheer happiness.

Eudaemonism, an odd-looking term and my favorite word.

V

Eudaemonism postulates that the only important thing in the world is to be happy. What leads to this happiness is acquiring knowledge about *the logic of being morally good* and then *experiencing the joy of doing it well.* Plato had it in mind when he declared that finding the nature of the good life is a simple, intellectual task, that of acquiring knowledge, and then that knowledge itself is virtue.

Good old Harry Truman was correct when he observed, "My choice early in life was either to be a piano-player in a whorehouse or a politician. And, to tell the truth, there's hardly any difference, and I, for one believe the occupation of the piano-player to be more honorable than that which occupies our current politicians." Ah! The talent to share words. Eudaemonism!

Oddly enough, even though not the president, I did once unwittingly play piano in a whorehouse. When visiting Havana—during Battista's time—as I was sipping some saloon rummy-drinks, I spied an abandoned, old upright piano near the *cuba libres* and soon was seated at the keyboard and playing away. No one paid much attention and, as the day and drinks continued their transition, I began to realize that the various women in the bar were regularly disappearing and later returning only to vamoose again, and certain gentlemen, mostly sailors, along with them. Now! What tune would be suitable for improvisation in such a bountiful brothel?

"After You've Gone" seemed right.

Today is purged of all clouds. Yesterday's continual thunder brought only brief showers. A flower garden basks in the daylight. The leaf of the main palm tree is making a face. What was only a rumor under the branches is now filling the tropic air with its secrets...and I'm stilll here wondering if the sun will send me to sleep. Perhaps eyes closed to muse over the recorded, musical choices in today's rotation: Adagio Karajan; Schuller conducting Schoenberg, Babbit and Stravinsky; Smith String Quartet playing Haydn 77 and 103; Zoot Sims and the Gershwin Brothers; Nikolay Medtner's piano concerto No. 2; Gosteleradio Quartet performing Glinka, Miaskovsky and Taneyev; Oscar Peterson accompanying the trumpet kings; and pianist Jane Coop interpreting Chopin. Music is so many things at the same time. Good, bad and indifferent. It is good to the creative writer, bad to the mourner and indifferent to the elevator operator. Meanwhile, wine ferments the music into emotion and ideas.

As Berlioz took many musical conventions well beyond their limits, he called his work a *fugitive* art. An example is his Requiem's delicate remoteness portraying the same musicking of a novelist: fleeting transitory elusive sprinklings. Fugitive thoughts, fugitive essays from a mind in carnival wandering, roving, vagabond. Very much present in the Fine Arts: *fugitive* color; a *fugitive* idea; the more tender and *fugitive* parts of the leaves; *fugitive* hours.

And now for fugitive literature, the falling away into fictional hands and existing in prose beyond any and all threats of failure, uncertainty and anxiety. With only the gentle wind as inspiration, writers can abandon their position at the center of the universe! Every author—successful and otherwise—should throw off conformity, go on an unpublished spree and take a stroll of allegation through some original *coup de theatre*...disappear into fiction…sit on the literary stage and see what it's like to perform in one's own opus.

I shall leave this cemetery of literary theories expecting to dance up some real demons as a make-believe character in my own novel. An autocratic Narrator forcing his presence upon a numbed population as they long for a fuller life. They must become autonomous then, no longer some aspect of their creator. My God! Is it so awful to be looking for people I have created who won't then reject me? After my goodbye to the publishing industry that has not paid my bills? I go out to this world as other gods of creation go to theirs.

VI

Here they come—all six—traipsing across the lawn—no wait—there's a seventh character gadding along behind. One I don't think I recognize. An extra, unidentified individual not imagined with the others. There's no mistaking the rest. It is my—good God! it is the role-takers. My six. The half-dozen vivifications. Occupants of my imagination now in awakened biography. Rich Freeman the humorist and Hirsch, his ex-wife ever on the ambush, the erstwhile priest and also Millie the egoistic, classy socialite plus the venial vamp named Doll. Ohyeah and forever groovin' is my jazz pianist. Stone: his lips form the constant wordings of bop.

Here comes the seventh person. The rest go on by. They don't know me. He approaches.

"Hello. We're just a bunch of writers on our way to the library where I run an AA meeting for them," spills out of him. "Thought we'd take a shortcut across your place. Some reason. Can't say. Sorry. Just call me 'Host'." He's British. Eager face full of smiles and a rather large nose.

What? They're all drunken writers now? What's happened? I see them strolling off as if I'm watching them in a movie. I blurt out, "Are you, uh, what are you, are you all problem-drinkers then?"

The man's grin is steady, effortless. "Yes, I see what you mean. AA. Alcoholics. We are the other AA. Authors Addicted."

"Addicted. You say 'addicted'?"

"True. We are recovering from scripturgia. The urgent need to be writing all the time. Pendependence, we call it. So many authors today can't stop or won't. They're in the anxious tense. But there's no problem with my guiding people who want to quit writing." He hesitates. He seems wanting to help me with something he can't express. He takes a deep breath and holds it, lungs working up for something new. Even so, his airy look summons me to my quixotic pursuit. He asks, "Would you care to stop writing with us?"

"Yes. I'd like to join you. Sounds, um, 'interesting'?"

Does everything start now? Entry into the clamor of freed creatures? gone into fiction a new rush of time. can't lose if this is all there is that's keeping me.

"If I could simply sit by and just quietly monitor your session."

"Righto!" He shakes my hand and then keeps hold, actually helps me to my feet.

This is it then. I'm going out to meet myself! We follow a little behind the gang of six and begin our stroll along the neighborhood roadway. I hear their chatter but I can't identify which of them is talking and occasionally laughing as I have never described their voices. And almost in concert, the miscellany of trees and sky and even all sounds seem unusally emphasized and fictional.

"These characters are quite an assortment, " he says. "Some talented. Some just charming. None shy amongst them. Villains all! " He's amused with this coterie, knows them advantageously. Will I as well now that they're at large? Or has this guy already ransomed them from me?

"What do they write about?" I'm asking him. I realize I do not have the vaguest insight that they would all become 'authorholics' and right now are trying to quit.

"You'll see," he says. He keeps watch on the moving *milieu*.

"Well, how do you manage them or, uh, improve them? I mean, how's it work? Are they all writing fiction?"

We're casually catching up to the others; so he stops our own advance. His eyes close. The arch look disappears. The nose seems larger. He seems to be waiting with deep thoughts. One comes out. "The writer either aspires or inspires." Now the eyes open to see if I am capable of following his rhetoric. "The first thing an addicted author feels is the silence of literary art," he begins. "Silence fiction." He observes me intently for any suggestion of appraisal. *Silence fiction.* I am terrified I will fly apart with laughter. I hold in my breath and do my best to mimic his wise looks. I concentrate on the only thing I know is here I am. Myself into my own fiction. Trading my freedom at last. The author in search of six characters. Now I discover them and, as soon as the objects of my disposition are bidden to take on a life of their own, they break free of my fantasies, no longer some aspect of mine.

He glows with pedagogic ardor. "Generally, addicted authors are soured by a grudge against publishers or else they are ruined by the secret truth regarding their talent. This is the kind of information that can discourage the craving to write. We call this disease "Scripturgia": a constant, raging need to spill the ink, as it were.""

Our stroll continues. I can't think why but I am hearing symphonic snatches of Dukas' "Sorceror's Apprentice" in my head, and its theme reminds me that I too have unleashed forces I can't control now. Is this man Host my exorcist?

We are close behind the others now as everybody carefully crosses the main highway and heads toward a huge, public-library building. Inside, the shelves practically smirk their extravagance. Novels, poetry, theater, sculpture, dance, music, architecture, biography, langugage...what a *mise-en-scene* for all of my plagiarism come to bear.

We're moving away from the books to an exclusive side-room and a blond-wood conference table set up for their session. Once within, the cast sits all round while I abstract a chair for myself just far enough from the table. Host is now seated on a stool a little bit elevated from the rest.

And it's Host to mention quickly that "This gentleman wanted to audit our class today. He is joining us for this session. Incognito, as it were. Maybe he will want to preside some day over a recovery program for another local group just like ours dealing again with the scourge of scripturgia. Maybe he'll learn something. Uh-huh-huh-huh... from our little conference."

How discreetly this man seems to accept my purposes as he unwittingly camouflages my intent! He stands away from his stool and at a small lectern. "How do you do? How do you all do? Quite well, thank you very much. When we're writing, it's always somewhere in bloody hell, isn't it? You can burst free though, you see. " He glances around. "Is any of us still writing? Milton once called it 'confusion worse confounded'."

Host now lectures eclectically on, ubiquitous about something the others are considering. I realize I am hearing all the words he speaks but none of the sentences. "*.....and then by Jove when the readers deign to provide their looking-glass*

*of approval perhaps we here are destined
to endless research with no need to write
beyond today you see there is no stopping
not whilst your created characters exist
think of those little tentative notions in
the mind where all is fancy...."*

As he strives further with them, still beyond my glossary, I am completely and utterly infatuated in the presence of my characters that I am capable at last of visually appropriating my six somebodys: their looks, their attire, their remarks, their sensitivities. Even their mirrors are mine. I'm *pro tem* them. In this way, these created *personae* are emerged from their previous portrayal in my published short stories. They are the prima donnas now; I, the lone operatic harpsichord between their arias.

Regarding this moment, I find them to be completely absorbed in Host's continuing observations. *"....it is not reasonable to cooperate in a society that demands too much from its writers regulated as it is toward complete orthodoxy and as we have discussed orthodoxy is the death of philosophy....."* No one is taking notes. But then that's the point if they are to be recovering scribes. Placed before them on the table are quantities of reading material. *"....and to depict something is to control it but don't we lose all of this control then if we have conquered the need to depict....."*

The nearest-seated character 'Doll' looks up at me, offers her most fascinating smile. She is the pimpette from my old, published short-story called "You don't Want to Be Me." (about a pull-string muppet suddenly spouting sophistry.) Her eyes have been brushed with copper shadow. Above. Not below. Her expression is saying here I am, and what are your other two wishes. Now she hands over to me one of the pages from the pile in front of her. Her fingernails are the deep, rust red of a Cleopatra. She absolutely does not sense my identity. Why am I expecting anything else? She tactlessly lets slip loose and so falls her sheet of paper which slides a few feet away and under the table where she sits. We instinctively reach down together. Immediate eye contact. "You smell like someone who has really lived." She breathes it softly,

The stars have lined up for some earthly mischief since I originated her. I put lots of summer into this little creature still hot at unshackling everybody's morals. Her look—("Have we ever touched?")— is pondering a kiss. I slip back into my seat and manage to stare down at whatever she places before me, wants me to read. It goes, *"Not all psychopaths become killers. Some write. One just wanted to write about me so I thought why not do it myself. I won't send anybody away just to find other cruelties. Watch me. Live me. I'll show up with words. Listen to consonants. Lie about vowels. Brush off commas. Cheat at spelling. enuf thru tonite tho thanx."*

Host glances at our small, whispered liaison but talks on. His demeanor plays up the usual sense of an Englishman's reticence about any show of feeling. *".....realize the danger of blurring prose based on the preoccupations of life the seed never explains the flower.....the great Bunuel saw hell as an absence of Divine light......"*

Doll then, with a toss of the coif which is instantly restored, shapes herself back into the chair. She is wearing two shades of blue. Big, white buttons. Her prettiness lingers at the pre-40 mark, many big moments on their way. Host's enthusiasm is now trained directly at her. *".....we go back to the beginning that self-contained egoism of childhood so much power and we can only keep it going by a dedication to writing writing down our lives our losses.....but who has written the words THE END? Who will do it?"*

He lets out a little rueful cough. Then, he says to her, "All right, Doll. Let me ask you. In the process of self-control, you really must be willing to take the most incredibly extreme risks. Did anyone ever tell you that?"

"The wrong people always do," she sighs.

With this remark, all the men at the table are utterly lost at her borders as though they have never seen her before. The oldest one, a retired Monsignor stands up to speak. He's from my short story, "That Was Yesterday," (about priestly pedophilia inciting a wave of clericide). It is a husky, tragic voice. "My name is Father P and I am a recovering scripturgiac." He is the perfect version of the Slavic sermonist. All gray hair and massive duty. A figure like a beer barrel. A face hard and serious with its watery eyes weary from too many discoveries. Despite his magnitude, he is tailored perfectly all in black and without collar.

"My addiction is writing what I call 'letters to God' and I get published in *Commonweal* which is the oldest Catholic journal of opinion in this country. I guess I like contributing and they encourage me because their intent is to spurn sectarianism and religious dogmatism. Anyway I used to send in poetry but most religious verse is so bad, Lord help me. I moved into mysticism aaannnnnnd into wonder and awe, faith and concern. And insight. Into the mind of God. That stuff. Like God created the earth out of a sense of cosmic loneliness. See what I mean. I can't, uh, I have to write about this. Then I get guilty of self-adulation and vanity and you can listen to this boasting even now. Only the sacraments save me but the minute I'm through with the meditation, I am sitting at the computer." Sighs. "Does God want this from me or shouldn't I be doing good deeds? I can't pray all the time and so there I am back writing again."

Host de-cocknifies his speech a bit, his face shiny with delight. "Writers' addiction is very difficult to predict in the long run even though we can isolate most of the factors that cause it. The great Edgar A. Guest completely gave up writing, declaring self-control to be merely a matter of philosophy."

"I know," says the priest. "But I am struggling with these many abstractions. All they do for me is that they excuse my actions and blind me to my failures. And yet. Every writer wants to cure something."

Now it's the character Stone who speaks up. "So that's what I'm saying, padre. Like you know change is so definitely on, man, like it's cool." He's the jazzbo pianist in my short-story "Note" (about the stuck horn in the deserted delivery truck.) His name goes with him like the stone's throw he is from that falling rock of cascading keyboard arpeggios. He is the stone skimming the water. He is the vernacular stoned of any musician. He goes: "Even the chameleon the animal if he's blind, man, he can still just change himself to match the scene even without being able to actually dig it. No eyes, man, and the lizard dude still does his thing!" Stone is awkwardly tall, a weedy-looking, blond horse-face of a guy, directionless hair growing everywhere except over a face where the color has faded out of all his features.

"Change is cool. I've had a lot of bizarre shit freaked into my skull like I'm one bong short of no brain cells at all anymore but if you can't change, like I know, like you won't win. Because, same as the rest of you cats, I am major into this. I can't stop writing far-out lyrics, you know like the words that groove with what I hear my brain is doin' when I'm jammin' I'm backin' everybody up or even when I'm solo, I hear words I got to stop playin' and write them down so I won't forget 'em and if I keep writin' I don't play so much anymore. So I got to quit words. Cold turkey, dude. The blues, fer sure."

It's Doll saying, "Why do you people write such lousy music for the porno films then? I have to watch so many of them just to make a living." She gives her hair another experimental touch. "I actually hate porn; but the money is always great." She is looking full at me now. "My face never tells on me," she says.

Doll now announces how she knows the dynamics of the mating game, "…especially when men think they want to change." Wherever she is, her sexual electricity is a catalyst. Her effect on women is only a reminder to them of lost time. She's not the old Eve, wasting an apple on the wrong person. She's the one who won't reveal a single thing about sexual mysticism. When life is less, she's the one with two mouths.

She doesn't really have to do or say anything. The men are absolutely possessed with her. Stone is forgetting his lyrical hopes. The priest wonders about his gayness. The third man—the one I named Rich Freeman, the professional comedian featured in "Now showing" (about a serial playwright)—sees Doll as yet another girl who will sleep with him just to get the free T-shirt. (I well wrote their fancies long ago.) His time as a comic has taken him from night-clubs and television to writing humor. He wisecracks through every occasion. A woman laughing helplessly is almost a sexual experience for him. His clothes and his hair also bring smiles of disbelief.

Host is saying something with the word *"rational"* in it.

Freeman, the stand-up, interrupts with his usual, comic-chance opportunities for humor—an unwitting straight-line from someone, a vulnerable target, anyone's personal imperfection or a handy prop—"…and who wants rational?" he says. "A comedian wants laughs. You know, like did I tell that I've been receiving ten enlarge-your-penis ads every day! And they're all from my girlfriend?"

There's no pistol-shot of comedy-club laughter but they are all chuckling. Except Hirsch, the former wife of the joke-teller. This imperious woman has heard it all before. And following up the ex-husband on cue as if instructed to do so, she chimes in, "Careful, Host, or he'll take over. He's dying to do it. Give him a straight line. Try to insult him. That's all he needs." She is not on good terms with any style of dress. Flat and mask-like, her face has the elongated, angular, Modigliani, surrealist look. Asymetrical eyes, thin nose and tiny, pointed lips. Deceptively fragile and full of discontent. She practices being the cold-proud woman that might cause a weak man to need her.

And she pursues this former spouse in constant inappropriate euphoria even as she is still falling through to her lost place in divorce. Off-key behavior accompanies her symptoms of irritability. She disregards Host's presentation—even the resulting flow of conversation—and begins talking. "I don't seem to be anybody anymore," this being her pettish and most frequent rebuke to Freeman. "My once-husband here has made me co-dependent to his addiction. I make excuses for his excessive scripting, he calls it. But he still can't stop writing wisecracks and trying them out on the phone all day and I'm talking about insults and smart remarks for anyone everyone he might meet. An offensive remark a day keeps his nose in Roget." She smiles a bitter, pinched look. "I wrote that and there is no trick to it! All he wants is freedom and look how lonely he is. So I go to Auddico." Her eyes become slits, and she slowly repeats the word.

"Au-dic-co? 'Authors Co-addicted'?" she emphasizes. "And they help me cope. I am completely dependent on his scripturgic behavior. Auddico tells me I'm now his enabler." She makes it seem that only she knows him so completely, and he just doesn't see it.

Host is the soul of patience. "We know all about co-dependency here. Good job that Auddico is helping you. I'm not altogether sure that we have the help, uh, the relief you might need today but anyone is welcome."

"You are correct, sir" she goes on. "I do not myself suffer from the scourge of scripturgia because I am not in need of spinning out a lot of language. I never was. Unlike some people! You see, I can take on a written communication or leave it alone. No effect if I never write again. Or do. Write." In a kind of anguished pleasure, she flashes her little teeth in an oval smile. "Listen to me. Not him. Not the goddam 'let Freeman ring' stuff. He said I cleaned the stove before I stuck my head in the oven. Is that nice? Well, he has this great appetite for the ladies. Has his own scoreboard."

"But, Host, dear," says the elegant woman at the far end of the table. "Aren't we all paranoid one moment and then cured the next?" She appeared in my story called "Scattered Crayons" (a sexual mystery). She projects the self-assurance of a classical actress, the kind who could play Ibsen or Zola, or someone who would be well-known for her tempestuous love affairs. In actual fact, her real life is domiciled in wealth and circumstance. She is heiress, muse, political idealist, refuses to be defined by her glamour or, for that matter, by the riches she enjoys. She is styled with a wavy bob, cropped to fit handsomely, *au courant* in dress and manners and literature, a bit snobby but warm and passionate in her addiction to seeing her by-line on the op-ed pages. She exudes the *cachet* of a woman known for writing her opinions. Named Millie for her "millions" when a million or two would mean something.

She is saying, "We are here to cure ourselves of the scourge of script. If only we are up to it, then we will abandon this, umm, this gentle calling. But, mygod, won't we suddenly just start up being creative writers again when our society keeps coming apart? The end of a great civilization is always just the right time for fiction. Somehow one looks forward to the fall of a grand culture because it gives us such inspired art." "

"Blimey, you're right. When the old England at the end of the nineteenth century declined, along came Dickens; when Russia fell on its arse, there was Tolstoy; when opera plot-lines needed some intrigue, it was Beaumarchais." He sings: "Don't... forget...Figaro, Figaro, Fi—ga—roooh!!"

It's Father P who chimes in. "I can say that the greatness of a writer is in direct proportion to the power of his country. Galdos, for instance, is often as remarkable as Dostoevsky but who outside Spain ever reads him?" He slowly lifts his hands in an episcopal gesture. "You know, now that I mention him, it feels odd to realize that some of those same Russian characters reappear in many of his novels. Oh, dear. This gives me an idea for a new homily. Good Lord, I'm never gong to be cured"

Millie smiles her cultured best. "There is a marvelous luxury in addiction. When we blame ourselves, then no one else can criticize us."

Host says: "And there is the cure, my dear Millie. After these sessions of defining ourselves in terms of our pens and keyboards and our computers, we now need to figure out who we are . This way we glimpse the antidote for disturbed scribbling. I find great personal comfort knowing that the celebrated elite of Britain have completely given up all authorship in favor of the grand, aristocratic art of doing nothing."

Doll fidgets in her chair. "I must be cured then. I do nothing. Well, nothing but write porno screen-plays all day. I bet it's over a couple hundred. Somebody picks 'em up. I can't stop writing them. They're always in my head. I'm, y'know, I'm really doing nothing, just like you say."

And so they are as I hoped, and thus they exist. My Six. Doll the coquette, Father P, Rich Freeman the comedian, Hirsch the ex-wife-in-pursuit, Millie the doyen, and the jazz pianist Stone. Everyone's psyche is in a sprawl with author angst, the compulsion to write becoming more obsessive by the passing moments. Host glances solemnly at each one of them and then abruptly gives a small, qualified smile.

"We are here to deal with that infernal enslavement of incessant scripting and scribbling. I mean we are writing and writing and still writing until our very death. It's the fluctuation between writer gratification and writer purging. I call it mental bulimia."

This is too much for Freeman the funnyman. "Why not call it 'authoritis'?"

"Uh-huh-huh," Host being up for it. "Huh! Quite good, old fellow, but yes, writing's a disease of the imagination and writers need to hate themselves going on and on when everything is all somewhere else. Think of Beckett. He was an obsessive. Like ourselves. Beckett was not only addictive, he was a man who wrote in French when he didn't have to. We can surely agree he earned the right to be an incomprehensible esoteric if he felt like it but we have the cure for writers' addiction. We can isolate most of the factors that cause it. Which brings us to a twelve-step program based as it is on the, uh, the other AA recovery system." He raises above his head a small bundle of papers. "These are its words, the time in life to wrench your destiny into your own hands." His voice turns austere: "So burns......the pale flame...... of a new passion. Let us therefore recite together the principles of our new state of awareness."

VII

Host passes around a printed sheet to everyone. It reads:

GUIDING PRINCIPLES
OF THE TWELVE-STEP
SCRIPTURGIC RECOVERY PROGRAM

1. We obligate ourselves now to escape from the three devastations of writing: *publication, book-lovers and prominence*
2. We have come to acknowledge that there is no reason to share unspoken words.
3. Having written is good but any further writing is bad.
4. A poem a day keeps you muddling away.
5. We realize the importance of being able to create order rather than stories.
   Accordingly, we will:
6. cultivate a passion to change whiteness; paint something.
7. use the internet only for reading purposes.
8. sharpen pencils every day but solely to realize the importance of lead to a well-regulated militia.
9. escape authorship by becoming a mirage where other people get to suppose us.
10. stop trying to raise other people's standards

11. stop having conversations with oneself.
12. develop other weaknesses

The Six Characters together dispassionately intone the words as if reading aloud from a Dick and Jane book. Such dutiful recitation of the twelve-steps betokens their readiness to survive the grand, insane need to be dreaming on paper. And, as I listen, I am able to realize how they reify the perfect novel: one that I can live in, as my existent life is turning into fiction and my fictional life becoming the realization of fugitive writing. I have left the theater of the mind. Crammed past my immigrant boundaries. THE AUTHOR JOINING HIS CHARACTERS. Endowed with actuality, they would no longer see themselves as make-believe, moving through life in a fictionalized account. They have complete freedom to exist even now that I've confabulated with them. Myself the author no longer haunts the stage. I am the mask among these strange figments who have no want of me. Can ontological speculation be applied to made-up characters? God guide me through my need to put some beauty into this engagement. God help me past His other nonsense about who lives or dies and about disease and bad luck and despair and ritual.

Enunciating the last words of the twelve-step— "other weaknesses"—puts them to introspection.

It's a moment or two for brooding, and then Host goes on:

"We are all born addicted. Think of mothers' milk."
He looks at each face. "All right. It was Nelson
Mandela said that our biggest fear is not that we
are inadequate. What we really deeply fear is quite
the opposite. We are beastly afraid that indeed
we are absolutely, completely powerful beyond
measure. It is our light, not our darkness, that
frightens us most. The man who fought against
apartheid says this: that we ask ourselves, just
who am I to be brilliant, gorgeous, talented and
famous?" The gaze intensifies. "Actually, who are
we not to be?"

Stone still studies the printed program. "There's
nothing on this page about fear, man! Writing
won't kill you, will it? Looks around. Sniffs. "What?
Does everybody here think I'm just one of those
druggies-at the-video-store?"

All present wait for it. Freeman takes in some air
seemingly to let out some automatic riposte but
holds his fire. The bopster goes on, "I know a word
in Japanese. 'Omonco.' Means 'screw you,' as a
Malyasian waitress once busted my chops with it
and then translated it by giving me the bird so I
knew what the bar-chick meant. Anyway. Came a
time I got to use this un-cool name *omonco* once
sitting at a sushi bar in Toronto. There was one of
those way-up-there, rice-cookin', land-of-sunrise
chefs serving snooty shit at the counter and didn't
answer me bitchin' about the yellow-tail he was
preparing. Pretendin' he was too hip to accept my
English. So I got him with that good old east-of-
Suez fuck-word. Everybody else working behind
the counter jumped up too when they heard it.
They all came runnin' around breakin' out their

coolie sounds. Course it was also me falling in and outta different rooms of dreams, you dig?"

Host's forehead wrinkles into an alert, critical expression.

"Hmmm. Yes. Good job that you came up with that, Stone. Well. So. This illness of writing must be treated with literary sobriety. Otherwise, it's all a load of codswallop, my dear chaps. Of course, you may know that you could just go on being dependent or…" glancing to Hirsch "…co-dependent. But *cui bono*? Whom does it all benefit?"

Hirsch immediately interrupts, "Ah yes. Working for a better yesterday." She seems to have memorized much of what she says. "You writers! You can only be what you are meant to be. I just don't have the ego and not the sob story that goes with it either. Freeman here is a compulsive die-hard always on the hunt. 'Corpsing' is what he does. Right, Rich? C'mon."

"What's corpsing?" a few of them chime in.

"Corpsing. What they call 'cruising' after 65."

"See? That's my joke," says Rich. "The broad still breaking into my act."

"Oh, yeah? He told me all he ever really wanted was a naked woman who would like lie to the police. Isn't that disgusting? He actually said it!"

"Is that so terrible?" he asks. "This refugee from my former life. How the hell do we know who's running that projector in her brain?

Hirsch's mood and her tone turn soft. "My potentials were always liked. My husband's gay friend one time years ago looked up and saw me moving down the stairs in our townhouse and he immediately said, 'She should have been an actress.' It had to be something in the way I descended. I was damned good-looking and a dancer, too." The others are attentive; Host with eyes closed. "I'm not paranoid," she insists. "Anybody, somebody out to get me has got me already. Planet Freeman. My time in therapy is just a place. I will lie down and the doctors aren't there." Her elongated, angular body-lines look cubism-come-to-life. "This place is cold," she announces in a whispery voice.

She pounts her lips into a wry, little dot, waiting to pronounce a "W" word. It comes out: "Watch," she says. <I'm right.> "I had to be the mirror of his disease. Freeman wrote his jokes every day all day. Soon I too had to write. About what, though? Authentic. I wasn't authentic. See, I am not getting any of the drift of a real honest-to-crap scripturger."

Host curls up his face at her. "*Scripturgiac.*" He prompts her again. "Scripturgiac? Yes? Umm, uh, withdrawal from the literary scene is painful and perhaps even dangerous. We are as Sartre's sovereign man and woman, condemned to be free but nevertheless ennobled to live in freedom as a daring quest. And so we shall find aesthetic merit elsewhere. A writer needn't always write.

He finds new wine, works on something else. There is acting...music...painting...architecture... spiritualism,...movies...parties...food... conversation...and even—bravo!—the cup that cheers."

"And what about sex?" Doll speaks up immediately.

Host considers this. Then, " Yes, sex. Sex would qualify as anti-literary, wouldn't it?" He winks his mellow acknowledgement.

She keeps on. "Remember in the flicks when Meg Ryan did that fake orgasm in the restaurant, and it was the only part of the entire movie that everybody talks about."

Freeman can't keep quiet at all this. "Yeah, I saw one of your own precious films. 'Lust in the dust.' Was that it? You were Darla the hooker?"

"Maybe. I did a lot of porno. Call it high-class coitus. One time I came right through the lens."

HIrsch is wide-awake to this. "Is that what they dooo?"

Doll rolls right along:

"I wish I had never learned to take off my clothes. And the only way for me to quit was to get on the other side of the camera and write porno plots and what is called cinemasturb set-ups. They shoot their high-definition video in a maximum of 16 days, you know. And, well. Okay. Well, now...." her breath slightly tremulous as she takes some air in, "I can't stop writing. Every day another script. It's better than faking sex, and I get paid just sitting around my computer all day without even changing out of my peejays." She flashes her *caliente* look. Then, "But no! No more being photographed to death. Men's breath in my hair! Their skin absolutely everywhere against mine! And I'm tired of taking showers. So that's how I became addicted." The others stare at her. They wait for more. "Okay I was in a rock group, too, for awhile. 'Sacred Snatch.' You may have heard of us. We were off and on the charts. Sooooo. Now I've got scripturgia. The word sorta wants to sound like 'scrip-CHURES,' doesn't it padre?"

The priest remains transfixed. Can they both actually have the same disease?

"So. Mister Host!" She's still on. "Will you cure me away from writing raunch? Where do we start? Do you want my age or my body marks or my information? What's the delay? Is there a gangplank somewhere that needs painting? What?"

Freeman laughs. Host says: "I guess you could call writing for film a form of dependence as bad as anything else. Some creative writers simply die because scripting is all they could do and without recompense, too. Well, poor Oscar Wilde died in, uh, in 1900. He had all those legal problems to deal with his homosexual misadventure, passing away in what was a seedy, little, beastly hotel. You know," he chuckles, "You know, even on his death bed, he looked over at the tacky wallpaper and remarked, 'One of us has to go.' Ah, the tragedy of perfection. You've all been published, yes? I don't know about you, Hirsch."

Her co-dependent presence does not validate her having any such actual addiction. She responds immediately. "I'm not here to be to be released, if that's the deal. I have no will to get away from writing I don't have to be cured of something that for me has no side effects. The chairwoman at Auddico tells me I have to stop—" she pulls out a pamphlet and reads from it, "The co-dependent has to stop...stop trying to cover up her...her... destructive habit. This means—let's see here— 'creating sustained consequences that will make him realize that right now his life is completely unmanageable. He must be reminded to give up his bad behavior and other choices.' There. That's why I follow him."

Host goes: "Ah, yes. The dance of anger."

Now Doll: "Do it, darlin'. I mean, a man is only just another domesticated animal."

Freeman has a face ready with retort. "They told her she's into the time capsule of luuuuv."

Father P: "But, Hirsch, perhaps you glamorize his addiction far too much."

Millie gets into it: "The gothic kingdom of depression."

Hirsch squints one eye. "What?"

"Yes. Depression," says the millionairess, regally beaming so glamourous a smile that the word requires a British spelling. "Remember this," she says. "Men all have one goal. Control. And women are their machines. I have had quite the gaudy life of courtship, and I have found a Mencken quote to be the best. 'Love is the delusion that one man differs from another.'"

"Ohyeahgirl, tell it!" says Doll. "There is something about men to annoy almost everyone." She shows off her smile of knowledge and information.

"I say, Hirsch," says Host. "You make a perfect catalyst for this group. You don't write. Yet you are compelled to piddle your time away in our little gathering. Might's well make use of your co-conspiratory itinerary. You have no fear of publisher trauma? The word 'enscriptment' means nothing to you. Correct? And you don't give a toss about writers."

The long, angular lines give her Modigliani face its gawky-pillar quality. Who would tell her that Modi is translated as 'cursed.' "I am still trying to locate myself, if that's what you mean," she says intensely. "You writing people always think like you don't owe the reader anything at all. It's so easy to see that you all hate yourselves. You! Are what goes on and on. And on. You can't be what you are because everything is somewhere else. It's like you're each swimming. It's alone. You're alone. Swim, write. It's the same. You don't speak, you can't hear, and you accept that you are by yourself. The world under water. A long long dream." The little mouth pauses as it spreads open to voice an N-word. And it is: "Neurosis. Yes, neurosis is inherited anyway. Did you know that?"

Freeman is ready. "Yes, yes. Being crazy is genetic. You get it from your children."

"Oh, yes," sniffs Hlrsch. "Well, let's not waste time here." She's almost aloof now, the empty, almond-shaped eyes and the tiny pursed lips, her face a mask feigning a desire to console, "I have come to get my husband. I will reclaim the Freeman forest."

Host gets up off the stool, closes his eyes to ponder for a minute, touches a finger to the center of his forehead. Then: "Hirsch. Your swimming thing is good. Let me think. Yes, there's a British writer and water enthusiast who suggests that the swimmer's solitary training, the hours semi-submerged induce a lonely, meditative state of mind. There is a wonderful abandonment you feel in water. It is so liberating. The writer's subconscious is the same, then. It is how you're just floating around and then sinking and then trusting the liberation at the surface. After all, we English know we're all of us going to be swimming for our lives someday sooner or later."

It's the priest now: "Swimming is by nature asocial. Why, the very substance of water puts you at a remove. And solitude is sovereign. When I dog-paddle about, the water can baptise out the concerns and anxieties of life…a sense of distance from it all."

Doll's in: "It's the way the water caresssses your skin, you know. You touch the face of the water and draw yourself so eeeeeeeeasily right across it, your eyes closed, and you reach as far as you can and then.." she pauses, and "..you submit to the strength of the flow and the current. Ahum!"

Host is back on his perch. "We are pen-dependents, remember. We're all in bondage here. And we need to rearrange reality: imagining, fantasizing, dreaming. Better ways to become fugitives from writing. We scripters deal with imperfections. That's what we go on about. Instability. After all, literature is just a war against cliches, isn't it?"

"Feels like we're here being x-rayed, you dig?" Now it's the bopster picking up. "It's like goin' to a shoe store has a machine that looks inside your foot to see your own skeleton. Everything's all there inside you but you don't think it is. Or you don't want to know it is. Even when you see your own bones, man. Now that's faith, you dig? And you are sooooooo silent, checkin' it out. Like you're back on training wheels."

I can see the Priest taking breaths into his system now that he hears the word 'faith'.

"I am into jazz, Mr. Stone, but isn't your music a kind of final push for inner freedom, I mean...."

"Just 'Stone', if you don't mind, reverend. It's more me than the name is."

"Gotcha. And what you say is that the dwindling possibilities of jazz itself have shoved you into doing some writing, right? More like how you feel in another scene."

"Cool and right on, pastor. Putting down a mouthful of words in some burning language is like a New York City overdose. Nome-sayin'? A computer keyboard same as a piano keyboard only the cyberspace notes are already there on the keys. Written down for you, dig?"

"Well, I…."

"And now, el dude Host is gonna throw out my readers. And me with them, okay?"

"Yeah, you need to quit," says Freeman, his eyes closed.

"Well, but he's in a triangle," comes Millie. "Sartre says hell is having three things in conflict. No resolution is possible. So music and writing and being high. That's you."

The straight-to-the-screen dialogue continues.

Stone: "I'm just tryin' to get the joint jumpin'."

Freeman: "Hey, I know all about it. My son is a beeeeg doper. Can't get off that junkie spoon he's on. Dresses like a male Shirley MacLaine, lives on macaroni and cheese, brings home comic books and thinks I'm stupid. After he's 'coptered in, he sits down, waits for me to speak and falls asleep halfway through the part about the police-car sitting out front."

Hirsch: "And, of course, you're blaming him on me again. How about finally taking that knife out of my back, huh? You'll probably need it again." She squints vilely.

Doll: "Men never get the point, dear. I can tell you if it has tires or testicles, it's gonna give you trouble."

Priest: "This illness of writing is a profound attempt to emulate the Almighty."

Millie: "You think God writes well?"

Priest: "God is an extremely uneven writer, but He's good." Looks up at the ceiling. "I, I mean, nobody can touch him."

A Few Voices: "Amen."

Priest: "God rested after the end of the sixth day. He was surely not tired. God resting means that He stopped his work so that man has an opportunity to have a hand in perfecting the world. "

Host: "That's good."

Priest: "And yet the books of the Old Testament do not contain any account whatsoever of man's philosophical feeling about God. That's something to think about, isn't it? You know, as a student at Oxford and writing poetry and romances for one of their magazines and deciding to become an architect, not a priest, and things always in a tangle, somehow I have some...if I have any power or calling, I would trace my journey to the priesthood right through the imaginations of architecture. The art of measuring things on paper first, this designing art that concerns itself only with those characteristics of an edifice which are loftier than its common use. And so a building cast up to honor the Creator is also of great benefit to mankind. Modern builders are capable of so much more. But.."

Millie: "Arthur Miller said maybe all we can do is hope to end up with the right regrets."

Host: "We are to coax scripturgiacs to try on the gowns of philosophers, psychologists, generals, actors and painters and, yes, musicians." Looks at the pianist.

Stone: "Heyyyy. Major underpaid, man."

Host: "Well then. We must now deal with other kinds of creative achievement. Rather than with the abstract constructions of literature. You know, point of fact, I want to wean you on the healing power of further arts."

Doll: "Is it all just our imagination that we can live another life? I would hate to give all my diamonds back. After I'm gone maybe but not a minute sooner." She glistens in sexual receptivity. "Death is for everyone else. So far anyway, right?"

Priest: "Death is delayed by love. Defeated by charity."

Freeman, into the elan of it: "Death is a big price to pay for getting God to explain baldness."

Here come the rest.

Millie: "I say death is taking its hilarious holiday called "Your Life.""

Hirsch: "It's just a city of lost machines."

Host: "Death is really a very small thing if you're a butcher.

Doll again: "Death is just worse lighting."

They are carried away with mutual amusement and as the merriment subsides, all slowly look at me to respond in kind. I think of my banal life in a retirement village and can only whimsically contribute: "Death is that chartered bus-ride where the bingo games slowly turn into prayer services."

The stares now concentrated upon me are positively crystalized as if I were that Grim Reaper skeleton-guy who appears in cartoons or Grand Gingnol or at any chance to horrify as the hooded scythe-wielder who is actually each doomed mortal's own death itself. Even Freeman the comic has no rescue-line for my little quip. Comedy is tragedy plus time. I ought to have said that. He who writes a novel is on trial. Twice: the expectations of readers but much more so the mandate of the created characters.

At least I have become one of them. Why am I thinking this? What are they saying now? Pianist, paramour, punchinello, priest, patroness and pursuer. All their voices come clamoring.

does   *WILL*   You know

it   WE BE DOING   I've tried

is God   **suddenly**   ART   and, um...

in any   **all**

of this   *Jive on, baby!*   **end**

Hear hear   *a nice*

my fine   *long*

mates: *coma*

don't
trip
over
each
other's
destiny."

Host's voice seems a bit tweaked by the outburst but where are they? Six characters loosened from some narrative register? Each is a writer and, therefore, a seducer and moralist, salted and sad in literary retreats. And myself no longer the Machiavellian—intellect plus force. Or, say, 'novellian'.

But apparently the library is closing for the day. Host is up. "Let us bring our reading material and adjourn to my digs. We may continue our session over afternoon tea." As he writes down his address, the attendees gather up their personals and exit the building. Host and I follow along.

They all crowd into the only taxi and take off—am I losing them? Will I ever see them again?—as the man and I wait for a second cabbie.

VIII

CONVERSATION WITH HOST ON THE WAY HOME:

"Well, sir, it's another day with these characters and I do regret I haven't even asked your name."

"I'm like Homer. I may not have existed."

"Jolly good then. You know, this is indeed a place for characters with curious names. My own signature—Host—is all the more intriguing if we examine the six persons in these sessions of mine. You see, the Latin word for 'host' is the word 'hospes' and from this comes the word 'hostage' as one might look upon our guests as hostage to their addictions and furthermore captivated at the very same time within my tutelage. They're voluntary, of course, but did you know that in the 1700s there existed a political practice of voluntary hostages?"

He pauses to direct the driver onto a country road. "1748 was the fateful year that English nobility volunteered to stay in Paris. This was on their word of honor, mind you, pending the restitution to France of certain of their North American possessions. This was a famous example that carried with it all the association of romance and noble behavior that often characterized the voluntary hostage scenario. And which certainly differs

from the cruelty and hardship associated with modern hostage crises."

I realize I am being evaluated to determine my capability of harboring any interest in this topic. I begin with, "That's a catchy rundown. You British have so much linguistic stock. Americans commit many crimes against the English language. We have almost a million words in vocabulary now. But the worst corruptions, don't you think, are the ones inflicted not by the untutored or just ordinary people but by those contemptible bureaucrats, the ones in government and business."

"And in academia as well," he responds. "It's the over-active *literati* that bloody well bloats the language to epidemic proportions. Yes, the bibliophiles, the pedagogues. They're the worst. Bookworms in charge of our speech and our vernacular. And just think of the pharmaceutical industry all those new drugs polluting the *patois* with such disgusting names. And the rest of science with a new star-drug and a new math and a new organism."

"And the more writers that show up, the more new words come with them."

"Precisely why we are here," he says. "The passage from author to abstinence comes when the scripturgiac finally realizes that literature is nothing more than silence carried to the extremes." His eyes fill with a mischievous light. "Remember the great Pirandello. Right you are if you think you are, don't you see." He taps on the window and directs the man at the wheel to a paved roadway.

"I always thought the British consider the valiant to be a person who doesn't have any ambition beyond his status. But you have to be positively heroic to give up creative writing, isn't that so? Is this what you're working on with these characters?"

"Bugger me, now you've got it! All this lot are *gallantes*, you see, struggling against literary dependence."

"I would think that heroes do not easily tolerate the company of other heroes. Especially not in fiction."

"Ah, yes, fiction. The world of make-believe. You can blame all such creative writing on the teachers, lawyers, ministers, tour guides, barkeeps, docents, matre d's, headwaiters and the audiences and the readers. Somehow, every minute, another novel swims up. Writers are always stuck swanning around forever in their *metier*."

"Well, what do you say is a writer then?"

As I query Host on this matter it is odd or is it my imagination that the driver slighty slows down the taxi?

Host clears his throat. "An author is someone for whom writing is more difficult than it is for other people."

The taxi resumes its speed. "I was in the middle of eggs and sausage when I thought that one up," he goes on, his eyes now dreamy-looking. "Aren't we getting hungry? I always say that Rome is the place for dining. Forget all those contemptuous Northern European menus. One wants fascism in the kitchen. Autocratic fare. Arabiatta. I was many times at table in *Roma*, my friend, where I ate without restraint; restaurants there are temples; chefs are priests. And waiters, the Divine messengers. Ohyes, and valet parking is wafting magic."

Is he off literature? "I would think an Englishman would favor his fish pie, a dill sauce, something creamy, pea puree.... a, uh, say a plate of tripe and onions...."

"Yes, yes, all such swill is fine, and it is indeed the menu they bring round in the pubs. But I'm such a left-over Roman. You know, restaurants were non-existent until 1765 when Boulanger started selling soup and the exact term comes from the word 'restorer', and that's what sitting at table is all about, don't you see? It's being in the just now, in the present, which is spoken, not written—uttered over *tira misu* and wineglasses and coffee cups late at night.

He rubs his hands together at the thought of this. "Too bad most folks are not a patch on this. They have become Hopper people. Those solitary figures in the paintings, sitting alienated or just looking out a window, all the pain from their lonely thoughts," as Host fashions his conversational way from late-night restaurants to the artist Edward Hopper!

"Yes,"I venture. "I do know the painting. It's 'Nighthawks', the other side of day, the customers in the diner, sitting at the counter. I think it was prompted by that Hemingway story about the two guys coming to murder somebody, wasn't it? Hopper said his consideration was more about predators in the night than depicting loneliness. He makes us wait for his people to disclose their own meaning."

"Well, my three lassies and three blokes may be a dodgy bunch but we'll have a bit of fun getting them into art."

"Art, you say? So then you believe the winning therapy for writers' addiction is to be museful? I mean, that these folks should have a go at another art-form entirely?"

"Exactly."

"Won't they need any skill then? Any talent at all?"

"Well, old boy, I'm saying whatever it is that displays form or beauty or...or unusual perception. No more plots or stories. All the physical artscapes await them. Rather than the dreary, abstract constructions of words, words, linguistics, acrostics, verse..."

"So you think things will hold together with this support group you've got despite all the neurotic self-love they obsess about?"

"Ahyes. The unique and non-stop repeatability of the written word as opposed to philosophy which tends toward generalization and abstraction and, um, such endless puling. Dead or alive, we press on with our little passage,"

IX

The taxi enters a lane that opens into a *cul-de-sac*, and there sit several houses on a small lake. We pull up to a bungalow affair that effects a second story look with a few amusing, Queen Anne stylings. What else can appear more homey for an Englishman than a faux turret, highly pitched roof and oriel windows...the purple prose of 19th century architecture! Alas, no wrap-around porch. There is a small front-garden given over to rose bushes. The six are waiting in the yard. We two alight from our vehicle and approach the thick door with its black knocker in the shape of a lion's head.

Inside it feels fusty even though the windows are all open, and there is the smell of lilac. We are admitted to a tiny parlor providing space for only a divan and a couple of overstuffed chairs. Onward through a sitting-room and the kitchenette and outside to the rear terrace where, past a modest vegetable garden and a small out-building, stands a great gazebo with all the exuberant sculptural extravaganzas of Victorian ornament: the cone-shaped dome with its decorative filials and the hand-rail enclosure. Perfect for hosting a social.

Indeed, we are breathing that atmosphere of innovation in which we all feel so at home. We take our seats at the oval table. At hand is a serving cart displaying a selection of quadrant-shaped biscuits, jam-pot, dessert plates, luncheon-linen napkins, creamer, sugar bowl and teapot covered with a quilted cozy.

It's Host: "HIrsch, old thing. Why don't you play mother and pour us each a cuppa tay." She lifts the bonnet and carefully portions all round from a Royal Albert, china teapot.

"Well, chaps, I'm happy to say that the scones are much better than the dry hardtack my Scottish grandmum baked, although the old girl did teach me to lift the saucer along with the cup. You see?" He demonstrates. "Scones are good with jam and then cream!"

Those present nibble their cakes, sip the strong brew as Host continues: "This is charming to be sitting down amongst such collaborators as you all. Let us test what we know and proof the coinage of what we have. You have written yourselves into a sort of bibliolatry. It's not that you worship books fruitlessly. We owe a great deal to bad books as well as the good, you know. The lesser authors and their commonplace heroes play so large a part in the silent-as-the-snow life of the writer. And then, at last, we realize that for us the novel has fulfilled its mission by a truly massive analysis of human feelings and motives extending over two hundred years. Don't worry. We were all young and knew nothing. Now that I am old, I love that in my heart I am still that same *naif*."

He stands, "Just know that you are not going to write today. "

Is he actually intending to disparage the entire integrity of literature? The arsonist of the imagination burning up the great essence of creative writing? The group's prized adventure-story treasures of today destined to be the cheap trifles of tomorrow?

"But enough prologue," he goes on. "The whole notion of literary *dishabille*—being stripped of that nervous incitement to write something—takes us to a higher kind of intellectual love. Start with nature, the conscious union with all that exists. Under the guidance of reason, we free ourselves from the instability of authorship. Meaning, we are jolly well off to the other arts."

The others have finished their light meal, folded their napkins and turned their eager faces into quizzical ones.

"Well, Mr. Host." Father P is first to speak up. "In order to be recovering scripters, aren't we sacrificing our literary refinement as well. I mean, if that's where you want to take us."

"Father, if I may," Host warming to this. "There is quite a prestige in art. But, of course, those that don't *get* art live on just the same, don't they? I don't know whether you're thinking of modern art. It's queer stuff when you first see it. Lights and colors. Patterns. Sometimes they're just geometric shapes. Who knows how far away from them you should stand. For me, it's the late 18th century Europeans. Elegance, harmony. David and Canova, you see."

"Well, Lord bless me," says Father. "I am quite weary of writing anyway. There's the note-taking, the memos, composition, editing, reading other's writing. Exposition. All the horrible literary theories. Plus, in my priestly case, I must take up the many other religious beliefs. I mean, I love my God but He will not release me from hearing about everyone else's." Father gazes piously beyond it all. Then, "For me, explaining the Heavenly Father has to be its own reward. And time is my ever remorseless critic. Ohhh, dear. Maybe I'd be better off as a simple atheist. Where you don't believe in your own beliefs. *Atheus detecti*. Oftentimes I am sitting outdoors and I feel gloomy enough to expect it to suddenly rain directly into my martini. No, I want some happy days, seasoned very much with a logical libation."

"All in good time," says Host. "We are done with the sitting and staring at a blank piece of paper until the drops of blood form on the forehead. . . That was a bit of the great Gene Fowler. Anyway, we shall transcend this world of literary impairment and try on the gowns of philosophers, composers of music or songsters perhaps or *danceurs*, actors, cabaret artists. Think mixed-media works, the animated film, poem-paintings. . .well, maybe not poetry exactly but if it's the word as painted, then. . .umm. . ."

Needless to say, his pause is what the company of six needs most at this moment. Outbursting with:

HE

WHO   RUINED   *Well,* I *came here*

  MAKES   MY   **love** *to kick it with Host*

I feel like **A** one-armed man in a second-hand store

  RELIGION LIFE   **performance**

                          art

not all **OF** us can be made of silicone

  ATHEISM   AND

          NOW

"The last touch of elegance is elimination, dear friends . Even if IT'S *yourselves."*

          ALL A BAD MOVIE

HAVE YOU ANY IDEA HOW MISERABLE IS THAT MOVING PICTURE ALWAYS GOING ON IN MY HEAD?

I'LL TELL YOU. (*It's Hirsch*) STAY AWAY FROM THE NEIGHBORHOOD WHERE IT'S PLAYING.

Millie tries a touch of understanding for the overwrought Hirsch. "My dear, the best love has no expectations. Besides, marriage is always explained too late."

Doll: " I finally had a first date with a guy who wanted to marry me. He picked me up and drove me to a restaurant but by the time he got us there, we had already broken up."

Stone: "Love is bad, man. Only the fanatics know how to do it."

Smiles light up the faces.

"I wanted to get you six into some of your previous poesy," says Host, "as sort of a farewell to the blank page. It's always better to live it than to write it, wouldn't you say. Well, I mean, I think we're straying away from our destinies. We've inventoried and catalogued each other to the utmost. And it is posited now that you have reached the stage of what we call 'literature without ambitions' so let us press on to arguing the way toward mastering your *froideur*, your fear of not writing."

"At last," mutters Freeman.

"Dearest scholars, you now propose to rearrange reality: imagining, fantasizing, dreaming with no further bondage. You become fugitives from writing. You are to sing, to paint or maybe just dig away in your garden and grow things or teach or travel, be lecturers, teachers, film-makers, actors, maybe a bit of intelligent hedonism, go to parties, keep up-to-date, adjust your nervous activity with some Zen," He likes this. "You will be able to spend completely fresh time to all serene and beautiful purposes. And think of it! You won't be missed! In all the indebtedness to the god of writing whoever that is, is there one? But no more prereqs that your sickness and your puny habit requires that you have this damnable propensity and know that your inked-out, written life is a flitting state, a dark tent for someone else's night!"

They all are stuck in silence.

"My God," sighs Doll.

"I'm done," announces Father P. "I am ready to cease writing and take pleasure in nothing more nor less than just buying something to read. You know, the best book to select is something you had no thought of owning, The extravagant extra when you go in to a museum gift-shop and pick up an unknown little volume on art, and when you serendipitously open it months later, brings for you that sense of a poet's life."

"I love what you're talking about," says Millie. "Surely I can go from journalism to some other extravagance. The only things that matter are art and beauty anyway. But, oooh, I can tell you, if I am to end my writing and take up something else, it won't be vocal music. And theater. The aspirin of the middle classes, someone said. Or was it me? So. Shall I paint then? Easy to pick up a brush, dip in, and is there some horror about finding out that putting color on things is not simple. *Trompe l'oeil.* The eye expects the artist to trick us into thinking about something other than ourselves. How perfect!"

"The world's too crowded," pipes the weed-killer. "Ef all writing when it's going to be that easy. What I like is being stoned driving on an empty highway."

Freeman ready: "And what you find out is you are still in the same, old parking lot, right?"

"The joke dude is slammin' now, man. Dig, I can't hang much longer without a hit, Homes. You know."

"Right, Stono," chirps the comedian. "I used to do drugs. I still do drugs. But I used to, too."

The Stone-man goes helpless chortling into the extreme joy of being understood.

Freeman keeps on: "You know, if we could just get marijuana into the mainstream maybe the other drugs would what was I talking about"

Stone now convulsive. Doll gets the chuckles and the rest are going with it, too.

Priest guffawing: "One of our deacons would get a little high. Ha-ha-ha. He was gay, too. Ha-ha. In fact, he was so homosexual I was worried for his own safety." Even more heightened hilarity all.

"UH-huh-huh now, father," says Host. "You know what they say about people who live in glass houses."

Freeman jumps in, "Yeah. People who live in glass houses have to answer the doorbell."

Hirsch not getting the quip. Not laughing either: "No one understands you, dear," the last word drenched in scorn.

He: "This woman. You know, when we were married. or say after we were married, she had all these mood swings, so one time I bring her home a Mood Ring so I can monitor all her many mooooods. And then guess what! I find out that when she's in a good mood, the ring turns green and when she's in a bad mood, it would leave a huge, big, red mark on my forehead."

Hirsch affects her little smile. "Oh yeah? Well, I know wherever my co-dependence leads me, I can either write or leave it alone, as they say. You know who I was married to. Him. The great, living, undeveloped, undiscovered and all-round unappecated him. That's the guy who can't stop writing down every *schtick* he gets to."

"To cease writing is not to lose all possible interest in life," Host responding cheerfully, Scripturgias don't even have to confess anything, unlike our alcoholic brethren. Right, *Monsignor*? Is that correct?"

"There is a kind of luxury in confession," is the priestly return. "After all, to put the matter to rest, the only thing penitents need is to feel we have been forgiven. I have written quite a bit about the church of Rome. It has not been easy on me, siding with a Christian persuasion that, more than the others, sees the entire world as fallen."

Not wishing to be presumptuous, I have mostly remained a listener through it all, waiting for my chance to get each or some of the six alone whenever Host tires himself or something calls him away. I'm feeling more like Godot as I practice my having abandoned these characters although Godot's creations failed to satisfy him. Not mine, however, my mind on my proteges even as Host goes on with his concepts. "…..*be the master of the language you speak, not its slave Those pages of yours will not save you. Perhaps because the good in them no longer belongs to any individual but rather to language itself. We move beyond that tradition with the utmost eclat*….."

The sixionals: has too much been crammed through their immigrant boundaries? What am I thinking about? Damn Host is making my thoughts become the same as his tortuous ruminating. It was my sense of the transcendent that got me to this company in the first place. Host goes on saying things while I evaluate my protocol "…..*as you imagists sign off it will be beyond this death of art and off to beauty-on-the-run a return to the other neglected vices everyone feel your lungs working up for something new and we have our monitor here whom I should encourage to speak to us begin with introducing himself and it should be of interest to get his reactions and so umm sir. Sir?*"

I should call my adventure something like extra-realism. Let's see. Extrism. Exterealism. Irrealism.

That's it. I should think about the falling away into fictional hands and existing in living prose beyond any and all threats of failure. Fugitive insolence on

"We're waiting, sir. Um. May we be introduced? I say, old bean. Are **you all right?"**

I'm I'm where the Christ am I? Ahyeah. It's actually Now.

"Oh. Um, uh, excuse me," I am stuttering. "My name is, uh, my name is *Storman. leo J.* Please just call me '*Story'*. Everyone does."

How-do-you-do's all round. A few with tea left raise their cups. I need someone to rescue me. It is Host with his own eponym to maintain as he says, "More on this gentleman very soon, I'll wager, but bugger all if we lot stay outdoors too much longer."

The sun is going down as a gradual scarlet-gold paints its tints on the windows of the houses opposite. I can still see there are reflections of twilight clouds on the waters of the complementary lake. The coterie departs our kiosk and strolls behind Host toward the residence. I stay seated just so. The evening wind begins to gather away all the shadows as nature exhales its exquisite timelessness. Birds will sleep away their nervous lives. God grants this moment.

X

A voice calls: "Story! Are you coming?"

I must go in. Finding out the truth about my players. That they are all addicted writers? What a discovery! The need to write is suddenly an affliction of the heart. Life has become something you write! Why not treat this truth with a little foreplay then. I confirm with a shout, "Yes. Still here! Thank you! Just enjoying a bit of...." The caller has gone inside. One last glance at the landscape. The colors are wearily fading out of things anyway.

"Come in, come in," It's Host at the door as I enter. "We're all wanting something to chill our intelligence. Have a seat and I'll serve you your first drink. After that," he winks, "you can open the sluices yourself. What'll it be?"

"Dry sherry's my usual downfall. I mainly drink the cheap stuff."

"Not here you don't, old fellow. Are you fino or manzanilla? Or Pedro Domenq? Don't answer because I don't have 'em. But I do stock some Carlos Primero brandy. I'll save a bottle for you to take when you leave. It's best served in a warmed glass."

"Yes, yes. My days in Barcelona or my nights really were always in company with Primero. I'd love some this very minute."

"Want it in a snifter?"

"Thanks. Perfect."

"Righto. Join the others. They are frightfully interested in you. Get their bloody little minds into one addiction to void another, you see."

"Over here, dear Storman. Yeah, I know. You're 'Story'." It's Millie, motioning.

"You got it wrong," says Freeman. "They should call you 'Stormy'. You are so contrastingly enervated, it's absolutely overwhelming."

"Don't confuse my being silent with being sullen. Our Host is now concocting my drink. You'll like me then."

"I like you now. Where the hell do you come from?"

They all stand around a rectangular, oaken table that is somewhat nicked and scarred from imbibers' abuse and now laden with drinkables, ice-bucket, glasswear and an assortment of chilled, raw seafood. We're in the library, creosoted-wood, ceiling beams, walls of books and art, occasional masks on display, also some pedestalled crystal. And a small, white upright piano waiting in the corner.

I go on. "I'm a writer, a life sacrificed to the never-ending needs of genius. No, Stop. Really. That's me being oratorical."

"Life is good," offers Host, as he hands me something olive-colored that he indicates is warmed.

"I'm not intellectual. I am not trying to mean anything at all," I say. "Just starting out and not caring. I guess I wanted to be a TV writer but it's just lots of hard work and then it is viewed and gone. So it was for me on to being a playwright."

Millie samples her champagne, "Well, say. All of us would make a nice, little drama for your quiet, little purposes, wouldn't we? You get to write a play about people who are giving up on the business of creating new sentences." The others fasten on to the budding conversation. "Shouldn't you write a play about us? After all, what's there for you to do when we all take up bird-watching?"

"Yeah, Freeman!" snaps Doll, as she scoops up some lobster dip on a cracker. "Whaddaya think about this guy?"

The jokester goes: "I donno. I've always wanted a job writing fortune cookies but I know I'd probably develop eater's block,"

"Good one," guffaws Stone, his mouth full of crab-meat. "Dig you cats later." Now he heads outdoors. He goes slipping out a side door after a winking glance as I spot him.

Host: "Father, you better bless this food before Doll here makes it all disappear."

Priest: "You can do your own prayers. I'm only into personal deliverance now that creative writing is taboo for me. I must say if spinning out literature is actually, completely gone, I will somehow find myself again in my collection of maps and hourglasses and my seventeenth century typefaces and, uh, the taste of espresssssooooo. Let's think." He closes his eyes. "What else do I still have? Word origins, Robert Louis Stevenson, Ravel, Bizet." Eyes open again. "Ohyes, and the church recently summoned me for a very interesting trial."

Millie: "Not regarding pedophilia, I hope."

"Well, let's just say people were waiting for my personal assessment."

Freeman raises his wine-glass: "Accordingly, ladies and gentlemen, I propose a toast." Glancing at Hirsch, "Although sometimes I think I've made one proposal too many."

She: "Little did I know the wedding ring he gave me was not a marriage ring."

Doll: "HoHO! This is getting good!"

Freeman (to her): "You should be in 3D. . . .that's my room number." He looks around. "Oh right. The toast. 'Now is the time for all good men to bed down bad women and somehow make them feel better after it's over!' Oh, shit. Sorry, Father."

"At least there's alcohol, thank the Lord," sighs the priest. "I once had lunch with a rabbi friend who inadvertently ate ham. When he realized it, he said to me, 'Well, father, it sure as hell isn't as good as women.'" All smile.

This is a cue-line stimulus for Doll. She twists slightly, image re-fertilized. "Lead me not into temptation, pastor. I can find it for myself." She gestures with instinctive, expected approval. I had written her to look good while doing bad. She continues. Let her talk. I've got to think. She's going so fast: "*...but not all women are made of silicone. And If you have to stand, you should be paid more. People who get to sit make too much money. I'm still auditioning to be me. And, you know, I usually got the part of the sarcastic prostitute and she'd always, she would always...*" Pirandello weighs upon me. His characters live a tragedy of unfulfillment. Mine are in a comedy of metaphysics. His creations, they all seek unrealistic resolution. My six are destined for their appearance beyond the short stories that I wrote them into. Ohhhhyes. Whatever I have, I'm stumbling into the fact that, after all, I've stopped writing just the same as everybody else. Aren't my little phantoms of art so very clever!

So here I come again to them: "Hey, according to Host, to write is to ruin life. And to write well is now up to someone else. Is that right, Sir Congenial?"

Host is offering around something from a silver shaker: "Against the slings and arrows of outrageous fortune, it's not so bad when they're only throwing the slings."

XI

Doll's in: "So, Mister Host. We are to develop an addiction somewhere else. Something way off in another place, correct?"

Millie: "Bill Clinton did it. After the Monica mess, he left office and became a successful statesman. Turned off one addiction and plowed right into— umm, maybe that's not the word—he matriculated into another talent. The art of hustling. All politicians are addicted to their *metier*. He sure ruined the democrats, though. Set things up for the republicans all the way to Obama. I met Clinton once at a dinner, and I can tell you the man's will to survive had an animal energy. But he didn't acquire—what can I say—he never achieved a tragic dimension. And as long as he appears untouched about what happened to him, we will never be able to figure out what happened to the rest of us."

Freeman: "Too bad he got caught with his pants down.

Doll: "Well, his fly, anyway.

Freeman: "Hey!"

Doll: "And Lewinsky blew more than the president." Her eyes go disoriented. "I mean, she blew some really heavy lifestyles for herself. Like gave up her chances. Imagine if she had just kept her mouth shut......I mean,......if...uh...she had...ohshit...I'm really blowing this...ohgod...I'm still saying it...."

Millie to the rescue: "There is something about a man carrying the world's ills on his back that makes us want to lie down on ours. That Lewinsky girl had the president absolutely in love with her."

A moment's pause and then Freeman: "I don't want to wait for love. I just want people's pets to. No, really, I am driven to be loved by everyone. Why suppose that people like me want to do jokes all the time? Humor is the lubricant of my life. It's almost a sexual experience when there's a woman stricken with laughter and helplessness in the face of a couple of gags. I made her laugh. She's going to like me. Or at least fascinated to death. "

HIrsch sets her glass on the table. "Divorce is an evil thing. It really makes you hate yourself for being unable to forgive yourself. Like that? At least I know what i've been disguising all these years"

"See what I mean. She's hysterical! I call her 'Strangella'."

"When he bores people at a party, he thinks it's their fault."

"Crazy women are part of my job description. Of course, the pay is lovely and the hours are good."

Stone re-enters now, making sure the door is slowly and firmly closed. I am again the only one noticing him. as Freeman carries on: "...and this woman, this former wifelet is the champion of the rights of nappers. Never far from the bed, and eons away from sex. Kind of a fortune cookie thing. Full of one-liners for the dead. A serious mistake in a nightie. The inventor of endlessness. And she's still baying for my blood!"

"Yeah?" Hirsch scowls out. "The land of the Freeman and the home of the grave! How's that, Morey Amsterdam?"

"Mygawd, she's right," he says. "I have donated my sperm, and we all know you have to enter to win."

Father P: "You said earlier you had a son."

"Nothing like the one you worship, padre. Just kidding but how ridiculous I feel in my role as a father. I know nothing so ludicrous as to see a grown man leading a child by the hand as they move down the sidewalk or to hear some guy talking about his children. 'My wife's children,' he should say. A male is an immediate stranger to his kids as soon as they are born. The infant is still just one of its mother's parts. The female has already known more about the newborn for nine months than the man can discover in a lifetime. When she reaches her teens, a daughter will see her father only as a possible physical protector and potential non-seducer. A son, however, will learn to be a rival as quickly as he can until he has children of his own and then he will understand his dear, old daddy but far too late. My own child from hell at thirty-five years old still lives at home even after I myself left the scene, delirious with divorce."

HIrsch glares her mental needles at him: "He's some father. Never on his son's side. I can tell you what he always is on: a phone, a barstool or a bimbo."

He puts his glass down on the great table. "Have I been a good father, a nurturer, or have I spent my time being a writer, developing my talent for comedy? Anything I write lives beyond me the same as an offspring does. If sonny needs to live in my former house with his old ma'am, then to hell with me and history. Hey, Host, what is this stuff?" He pours more from the shaker.

"That's what they call a sidecar. It's brandy and some triple sec and lime juice, blissfully blended," responds the counselor who has now brought in large servings of caviar.

"Ew-ew-ew! Sturgeon! buckets of it," squeals Millie.

Freeman cascades on: "I ran with the drinkers. Reckless with joy. Someone once called it intelligent hedonism. The booze crowd. Always ended up at some ungodly hour with a ridiculous and precarious situation like an impossible bar bill or in somebody's apartment or—God forbid—like driving home. You pull it off. A million hoots, jokes, quick goings-on, chickliners we called them, you're gettin' those interior laughs, no touch of futility or no realization of tragedy but oh-boy the drama. How many times have I lost track of a fourAM car in nightmare tier-parking, five blocks of combined and stacked auto cemeteries. Ah, the whims of life.

Lost cars and lost loves. Perfect for the drunken beauty of survival. What a faint interest we drunks all have. Like a clock saying STOP at every tick."

"Sounds like almost as much fun as weed," goes Stone.

Hirsch knows the pot-crowd her son brings home. "And that's the household I got," her eyes gleaming with these new words of self-insightfulness. "Alcohol and drugs." She looks the Modigliani's hyper-expressionist portraiture of inner turmoil. "Is this the place for me to say I've died but no death?"

Death. All immediately regard the clergyman.

"I should tell you something," he begins. "Maybe it will help us all. Because I am the lucky one here. For me, a retreat from the literary life proceeds quickly to theology, religion being the dreadful situation in which we find ourselves, you know, with scarcely a clue as to whether our existence has any real significance at all. Shall we pray in the howling storm or rejoice in the stars? He looks all around. "Life! But religion is about death. And there's where you realize you can pray for something all you want to but God doesn't take sides. The Almighty is only interested in keeping the created world in balance. That's what I write about. Or used to write about, yes? Host?"

"Heavy jive," says Stone as Host merely lifts his glass.

"Truth exists by its own majesty" observes Father P, looking a bit weary from all his phillipics. Yet: "But aren't we bored with worshipping that same old god of literature, that creative rival to sexuality? Ah me. And, Hirsch. Your name means 'deer', doesn't it? Are you German?"

"We were Austrian. And, your holiness, or whatever I'm supposed to say, you got either the priests controlling everybody or it's the doctors. I'm my own Judas, see," she trills. "Thirty pills in my hand every day as payment to my illnesses. Effexor. Prozac, Abilify. Seroquel. Thirty tablets that ride my veins. That's it. Thirty-odd pills that operate in not completely understood directions on neural pathways. No one knows why they work. Where do people learn all their authentic happiness?" She sounds her huntress self, "I can stare at a clock all day wondering about a world where nothing matters except the time lost when I'm fresh out of my own expectations. And. Of course, into someone else's."

Her glare flashes around the room.

"All the cats join in," says Stone.

She powers on, "Get it? Nothing! No, nothing happens until your clock strikes the time for you and you're crazed into puffing on whatever life gives you to suck on. Got it? I don't. So I wait for whatever will break through my co-dependency and this is my therapist's madness and her goddammed soliloquies. Even if there is nothing beyond the keyboard of life. There. How 'bout it, Stone?"

She exhales in what seems a great relief for her. The other two women shake their heads empathetically. Even Freeman who blurts out, "Well, I sure got myself involved with one long Jesus of a skirmish here. You try to live with a depressive who takes to her bed early every day. And she always needs a good reason if there's going to be any sex. She thinks where a husband comes in is when your romantic days are over. "

"Yes," she responds, "but I still know you can't be firm enough without my pressures on you and my interest in you and my knowledge of what you are at the moment. The doctors all tell me about another person's sensations. No. I actually mean, 'Another person's persuasions'." She selects a single, chilled shrimp, places it between her teeth. A quick bite. Serious chewing. And:

"You know who I was married to? It is the great, living, undeveloped, undiscovered actor, short-story schlemiel and all round spontaneous, celebrity psycho-talker in the city of Pittsburgh, Pennsylvania. On the way, he has combined the techniques of writing and philandering. And now in the clutches of scripturgia—which you must swear off, mustn't you, Richard?—you will finally know what it is to give up something you actually need. Besides me!" She pops in the rest of the shrimp. "I'll get you, my pretty, and your little dog, too!"— giving voice to the wicked-witch, raspy-throated, land-of-Oz-Margaret-Hamilton broom-rider. This as she suddenly goes from Modi while her expression becomes the confused, sad-looking portrait of the woman in one of Dali's paintings. No line or form, just put there in formulaic arrangement.

XII

The priest is pouring himself a Hieneken into a huge mug. "You know, Hirsch, the very first statement that God makes about human nature is that it is not good for His creations to be alone."

"Surely, if God exists, He designed us for trouble," offers Millie. "Actually I'm sort of a born-again atheist. I mean, why go through the entire Bible when the meaning of life is available in the first few pages."

"Which is?" comes Doll.

"The meaning of life is the game we have to play. We're all like Eve getting our start in Eden. Figure out the truth by eating the fruit on the tree of knowledge and use your brain from there."

"Too bad they didn't try the plant of ignorance," says Stone. He looks around. "Marijuana?"

"What can I tell you?" offers Millie. "God created woman second. Man should have been the cosmic afterthought. Not Eve. Not the Muse, the Fury. Our matriarch. The mother. Virgin birth, padre, right? But to stay with the story, God the Divine Father goes out and arranges the heavens and the earth and brings into being all growing and living things. Each and every artifact has been framed and consecrated and waiting for humanity. We begin with Adam One placed upon the stage of creation. And in this way, you see that now the Almighty gives Himself someone to talk to. And God places this first human in a great garden the man gets to live in while he's naaaaming all the animals! Then the Ruler of heaven and earth is about to take off, and He realizes—wait a minute!—there could be one thing He left out. Because what the hell Adam's all alone. He needs human company. Not just aaaaaaanimals. You could train a baboon, y' know, to do anything you want. But he still looks at you and thinks you're just another ape. Right? In the beginning, the Lord of Hosts forms the entire universe, earth, stars, trees, the waters, the weather, the human brain, time itself...and then, it's just a last little touch but how about, say:::::::a *housemate* for Adam. An accessory? A piece of lass! So what's He do? His dumbest idea: Adam is put to sleep and God takes one of the guy's ribs and bang! you have woman. Bummer. The idea should be that male and female start out the New World as being created equal. But, no. God was obviously so fuh-klempt that day that he just grabs a rib... no time to spare."

Freeman: "Spare rib? Is it the right moment for a pun?"

Host goes, "Have on, you lot. Conversation is the perfect antidote for writers' addiction."

Millie's expression is she has more. "I'm not done, Hosty-toasty."

"Yes, yes YES!" sings out Doll.

"So here's what I'm telling you," Millie proceeds. "God concocts this jerk Adam, and he can't even obey one lousy command. No! One simple piece of fruit, he couldn't say, 'No thanks, I don't want to spoil my appetite for later because I can have everything in the entire, fukeeen world for dinner and anyway, apples give me gas.' Instead: the pathetic putz absolutely just has to scarf up and then pretty soon, he gets the boot!"

Father P is enjoying this. "If it's any help here, the prohibition given to Adam not to eat from the forbidden tree produced in our first human this state of anxiety. Because Adam can realize the temptation to disobey and that there is the potential termination of eternity. No life everlasting. And so the temptation here to disobey is actually a seduction and thus sexuality introduces the temporal into Adam's life. Ah-men."

Hirsch chimes in, "So they left their Eden to face a life that was to be the survival of the less than fit."

"Good one, you," says Doll. "Men think with their blood. They start out insisting that happiness does not exist but that a very few privileged male souls will tell us they know how to invent it. And in ten thousand years, you bums have not been able to get women to do your murdering for you. As a matter of fact, in all that time, the best all you bull artists have ever come up with is the elimination of foreplay. That's so the males can spend more of their time giving us sermons, staring at our sex organs, attending our funerals and making sure we all have weddings and more children. We matriarchs are under the control of those individuals who, by normal standards, get very little love-making."

HIrsch raises her glass. "I am proposing a nation governed entirely by people who are not crippled by all those adulturous emergencies."

"Right! Matricocracy!" is Millie. "Free spirits who can have all the sex they want. Anytime they want. Wherever they want. Or not. This would, of course, be a world governed by women! WIMMENNNNN!"

"There aren't many women in jazz," goes Stone. "I mean, they're all singers. We back-up cats have to do the close-in, back-up language. Trying to sell sanity with a blank soul. Time's just notes and beats to us. We got to follow the listeners' payment. Oh, man, where am I? Hey, wait. But no. Jazz is just everybody gettin' wigged out on sounds. I'll tell you this. There are too many who want drugs. Like me, you and your mirror."

"Christ, you ARE funny," says Freeman. Stone puts his hand into a salute and snaps his finger.

Priest: "Well, you see, men are constructed entirely different from women."

"How right you are!" Millie is flying now. "Men can have one, single, solitary climax; women, an unknown number. That's why the macho race requires so many magazines. Porno shops full of thousands of centerfolds, millions of movies, marital aids, inflatable creatures, peep shows, cat houses. Sooooo much phallic rehearsal has never produced rational leadership. And the reason is you fellows have no self-confidence. You got no game, boys. But women! The female has that inner peace that comes from our total sexual assurance, something males have to function without."

"EEEEEEEyeah," goes Doll. "You guys don't know how to spell 'peace' with an 'E A',"

Freeman steps in. "But it takes men to build empires, conquer the barbarians and make the world safe for democracy. How about that?"

Doll talks through a mouthful of sturgeon. "Democracy was great during the five minutes it also meant feminine equality. Except…." She holds a forefinger up. "Except if God had been a female, do you think She would have made us out of some man's bloody, goddam rib?" She stares at the priest, who shrugs. Then: "The major part of being under one of those bastards is to be able to fake love. They want us to sound passionate and act needy and be overcome—now there's a word—they worship us for when they can leak a little love somewhere." She daintily pats a napkin to her lips.

It's Hirsch now: "Men are so intimidated by their sex drives. I really think most of them would choose to camp in their closets if they had the chance. And really, does anyone know? Can gay people be cured?"

"Of what?" goes Stone.

The priest in mock expertise: "It may surprise you to know that homosexuals can be cured of the exact same things that straight people are heir to."

Freeman is: "Good line, papa. I gotta write that one down. Uh-oh! What am I saying here! This is a fine comedown for a man who is trying to become the toast of Broadway or at least a cheese blintz. Here's a joke for you, Stone. First, I need a drink. Where is it?" He accepts a pour from Host. "OK. A very intense tenor sax player is sitting at the bar, coming down after playing all night, and an absolutely gorgeous and shapely young lady approaches him and says, 'Excuse me'."—Freeman does the high voice—"'I hope I'm not intruding but I must tell you that I heard you play tonight and I don't know very much about jazz but I've never been so deeply affected by it before. The way you play woke up my mind and my heart and it also woke me up as a woman. Your solos touched me deeply and I want to take you home and I want to make wild, mad, passionate love to you all night long.' The jazz-guy stares at her for a second and then says, 'Were you here for the first or second set'?"

Even Hirsch kind of hisssses out her amusement but Stone shudders with laughter. "Oh ho ho oh no ho ho no please no maaaaan laughing's the god ah ha ha the god of oh shit I am so trashed. I gotta sit." He glances at Host who points to an old English wall-chair.

He stays up. "We turgias should be like musicians, man, when they're jammin where everything is jazz, God, jive, sex, reefer, a little sauce maybe, some poetry it's hard to drink and play the piano the keyboard needs ideas from both hands runnin along the next chord change at the outskirts of your brain, dig, and a million synonyms for that love tunnel, you know?"

"You d'man!" says Freeman.

"The dude writes," declares Doll, immediately into the trays of munchies Host has brought in. "even if right now he sounds like he's had enough coke to powder the Alps."

They grow abstracted. *Good go. Do you think so? Have some. Try this. Host, you're marvelous. Come on, Story, fill 'er up* **And here I am, intruded within the six society of my impudent philosphizers first arguing about their intuitions and now taken to nibbling and muttering their way through the *hors d'oeurvres*. A break may be great for the change of art they are all fronted on to. Will they indeed opt for lecturing or painting or acting? Traveling? Maybe a *coup de theatre* where they combine their transient commitals. And the scripturgia. The puny habit. Haven't I given up my own propensity in order to join these characters? I'm certainly not ready to toss my dreams so that all the people disappear. I think of Emerson on writing: "Thou are sick, but shall not be worse, and the universe, which holds thee dear, shall be the better."**

XIII

"Try this, my dear fellow." It's Host with some shaved ice in a scoop and more sherry. "Enjoying yourself?" as we move away from the others. "I would never think to put ice in this drink. You Americans!"

"It's the palette needs cooling, not the sherry," say I.

The priest approaches us. "Well, gentlemen, I have decided to do the civilized world a favor and end my writing. There is a higher goal of spiritual living than tossing out paragraphs. And it's really a lot easier for me just to search my heart for the presence of God. Why do we write anyway? Isn't it just a compassion for others that we are scripturgiacs? Whether to inform them or to help them by writing at them? And so far as taking up art is concerned, it's all prompted by thoughts of God anyway. The early church needed converts so mentioning crucifiction was not exactly kosher. How late it was that the crucifiction was finally made important by art."

He smiles at this. The cleric seems to have smoothly forsaken his addiction but is loathe to be left to the mercies of religious doubt. 'The messiah will come when a savior is no longer needed.' Stuff like that.

My dry sherry improvises its mischief as I sputter with: "Well, um, the, uh, practice of celibacy would not help matters for you. I mean, such self-discipline and denial is a higher vocation, I know but. . ."

"There are many of us in the world who live without sexual activity, whether priest or layman or homosexual or impotent or however traumatized. Or just disinterest. I can say that the highest, divine type of man revels in the joy of living in the unexpected enchantments of love plus the cup that cheers, and, of course, song and springtime and victory over the enemy or the prayer of a saint, the call of a bird and the absolute loveliness of silence. How's that?"

"Excellent!" Host roars. "You're cured of everything now except Catholicism. Just kidding, old chap."

"I know that," crows the priest. "But how do I give up writing and go to art? I have taken issue on this with Catholics, Anglicans, skeptical French philosophers and orthodox Jews. They all end up saying God loves artists but is indifferent to art.

My sixologists are really in to it now, and so am I. When I'm drinking, it's me plus someone else, that far-out fugitive I always think I've lost. So. "Mankind certainly paid no attention to God's being apathetic about art," say I. "The human race holds the absolute, romantic belief that icons and paintings and exquisite mosques and beautiful carpets are proof of political virtue. And there is nothing about God the Author."

"You mean God the Author of all lives or God the Author of the Bible?" chimes in Host.

Their palates now assured that the flow of cocktails will be eternal, the others have stopped eating and begun focussing on the conversation.

It's Doll: "Who the hell wrote the Bible anyway?"

And Stone: "I like the part where Moses checks out the mountain-top and he sees God all day and he picks up on the Ten Commandments, dig? And he comes down and the, uh, is it, the Israeliters are all boogie-ing and partying out and got some golden calf dude and ol' Mose is definitely not down with all that and he trashes the entire list, man."

"Well," Freeman in fast, "you know the Jews and their dinner parties." He gets his laugh and goes on. "They were much better behaved at the last supper. During the meal anway."

Hirsch now: "Leave him to make a joke of the Bible. See?"

"What joke!" he barks. "There is absolutely zero humor in the Bible. Not a line of wit anywhere. The burning bush, the plagues, the ban on homosexuality......not funny."

Then Millie: "All right! No humor in the Bible. But God is farcical even when He doesn't mean to be. Imagine calling upon all of humanity and commanding that no one shall be permitted to commit adultery! No love affairs? Nobody cheats? So many wives, so much eternity. God can be amusing. He just wasn't able to do comedy. Right, dear minister?"

"Marriage is not one of my privileges," he answers. "But I could point out that God somehow created just two, a man and a woman. The rest of humanity then sprang forth from only the two humans. That's the entire race of man. But not so with the animals. The Almighty called the animals into existence by specific species. Not just two of a kind for one sensuality. He created the birds, He created the fish, et cetera. He fashioned a man and then a woman and then a family. Why do we suppose that is? Why is it that all living things were produced by species and man was created only as an individual? And the answer, dear friends, if you don't mind my opening another beeeeer......the answer is that God the Father arranged it so that every human being was to know that we are part of the same family, the successors to Adam and Eve. All of us a single breed and all brothers and sisters in our innate knowledge of the other guy's psyche. That's so no one will say, 'My blood is better than yours'." He takes in a huge draught of the suds as the ladies all lightly applaud his insight.

He responds: "Ah, yes. Thank you. There is one thing we all share with God. We love to take praise."

Host is mixing up a new batch of cocktails and shakes up the mess to a silvery chill. There can be no harm for my switching over from dry sherry if I am forced to it.

Priest carries on: "It's interesting also that the books of the Old Testament—I mean the entire Scripture from Genesis to Chronicles is nothing but a long conversation between God and Moses and then Moses to Israel. The entire moral teaching of the Prophets is not through books but through discourse. The more solemn term "communion" means talking to God."

"So who wrote the bleeping Bible ?" sighs Doll.

XIV

The clergyman glances about for a place to sit. Host points him, and the others pull some chairs in closer.

"How much of this do you want, dear girl?" He puffs up his cheeks and then vents a long sigh. "Well, 2500 years ago very few people could write anyway. So there was an oral tradition as well as the writing on papyrus and leather and clay. Whatever the documents were would have had to be passed down in oral form before being recorded in writing. And, in time, they had to do it all over again and translate everything. I don't want to get boring here. Aramaic, Greek, Hebrew. English. What a passage through the ages, eh? And, you know, translation matters, I mean, the creation of any literary transcription must be inspired and shaping, not a pathetic shadow. In other words, a new work. All to be at the heart of Judaism and Christianity. Jesus was not a Christian, of course. And he did not anticipate our Bible, the New. And what he preached was substantially at odds with our scriptural culture." The listeners are fascinated with him.

He takes in a great swallow of beer. "So who wrote the Bible. You tell me. Was every word dictated by God to scribes whose only function was to write it down in whatever language they used? Or was the Bible a few Divine encounters from those in their everyday lives who actually spoke to the

Almighty? Abraham and Moses. And Noah. People even today claim God speaks to them, right? But really. The Bible is just literature like anything else, isn't it? The Old Testament was written by persons inspired the way all classics are created. The same as great art and scientific discovery is spawned—from the wellspring of human genius. Here's where we need our atheists to tell us there really isn't a God and that it was all written by obviously brilliant thinkers and dramatists."

"Crazy, man," comes Stone.

The priest smiles. "You know, I love to meet Jewish atheists. Their very position that there is no God makes them even more Jewish to me than they realize."

Freeman is ready. "There was this Jewish atheist who was quick to tell you: my grandfather was an atheist, my father was an atheist, I am an atheist and, please God, my children will be atheists."

The wisecrack strikes the perfect regard. I can't help laughing the loudest. It occurs to me that the search for historical truth is just a big yuk anyway. Not faith as opposed to philosophy but rather a kind of inquest. After all, God created all those atheists.

Millie pours herself some more champagne. "I read that it's all archaeology. Good old scientific research getting into ancient cultures and not just to prove or disprove things but to find out what the manuscripts mean."

"I always wondered," it's Hirsch now. "how the hell did Moses receive the Old Testament which has the story of his death and he wasn't deceased yet, you know. How funny is that?"

"Groovy," says Stone. "No laffs in the Bible, fur shurr. But that Noah dude, man. Hangin' with all those animals. He talks to God? Dude, he could have avoided that whole trip. He should have just told God that he happened to be an atheist, right?"

FREEMAN
An atheist talking to God?! How can you speak to Somebody if you don't believe in Him?

HIRSCH
Married women do it every day.

HOST
Ah, marriage! The penalty for being male.

My turn. I'm feeling just a bit lofty. Maybe it's the Sherry AND the brandy. "Any such contemplation that God did not personally dictate the words in the Bible has always been strongly opposed by religious institutions."

"Ohyes," agrees Father. "Yet it is interesting that in modern times, Pope Pius XII encouraged research."

"Anti-Semitic bastard!" whoops Millie. "He was a font of indifference to the German atrocities. That guy was absolutely silent about Hitler. And here was the typical hypocrite. He turned down Jewish pleas for help, said he was going to be neutral about what was happening to all those souls. I read that the little shit did shelter a small number of Jews somewhere in all the *mishmash*."

I have to comment. "Some have argued that he was anti-Jewish only in the traditional sense of believing that Jews killed Jesus."

She glares at me for a moment. Then, changes her mind with a cunning, little smile. "Life has turned good for the American Jews and their many mistresses."

"You're Jewish yourself then, of course," says the Priest.

"No longer practicing, I have to say. But...." she does an accent, "Vonce a Yenkee, allvace a Yenkee, mein keend!"

"I'm somewhat the opposite of you," says Father.

"You're one of us?"

"No. Of course not, really. But you are a Jewess and not a worshipping one and I am Roman Catholic but extremely pro-Semitic. I should say 'pro-Jewish'. I just got kinda tired with the daggone Catholics eternally eager to burn heretics. At one stake or another. And everything's really so simple for the Jews. Just go for the all-powerful Jehovah who brings about the creation out of nothing, and we're all instant Adams getting our start with God

in Eden. Beautiful, huh? How bout it, Mister, uh....
Storey, is it?" He's calculating me now.

A polite, little laugh is my best beginning, "All you
six are so interesting to listen to. That's what writers
do though, isn't it? Off the page, you try to make
your conversational selves charming, stimulating.
You vie for attention among your peers. You trade
around the *outre* words and the *au courant.* Your
repartee is ripe. And now, in the moment for you
all, the very act of scripting must become like a
tedious irrelevance. So the whole notion of being
stripped of scripturgia is...........um"

Millie, Freeman, Doll and the priest: "Ye-es?"

"You're to be placed into an environment where you
are thrown upon yourselves. No longer vulnerable
to readers, for example. But what imaginings, do
you suppose, will come forth now in love of art and
creation and the rapture of self-exmination and....
and......" Damn sherry, what am I going for here?

Doll has finished her noshing and sits, long legs
crossed and herself beguiling. "Let's put it all
out there," she begins. "So. I have this to say.
My agenda from now on will be for me to look
hemispherical." She smiles at the full attention
she so easily gathers. "Men can circumnavigate
my waters, chart their territory, go down to the sea.
And like Father Confessor here I too have—presto
change-o—escaped scripturgia and am already
back doing the Doll number. As for my choice of
art—"

Her eyes narrow into slits of secrets

XV

"—it is sex, the language of power," Doll intones.

Every male in the room looks drugged in Kafkaesque concentration. What have they done with their lives that they so utterly do not deserve her?! Their thoughts of any social good seem drained out of their faces. Are they forever to speak only in some unused language or wear numbers on their shirts or keep chosing the wrong door? I wrote her as foxy, creative, amusing, philosophical, obsessive, flashy-attractive, indifferent manic. But not a needy one.

She's smiles demurely and: "I know that you writers just pick up a pen and a piece of paper and you can completely play God, can't you! And now Host declares you're going to be changing horses in midstream. But the horse has a rocket up its ass, right? Where's your horse-joke here, Freeman! Yes! And, my dear dear Pastor! What good is faith if you can't compare it to sex?"

"Lord save us, you've got to explain this one for me," says the wide-eyed priest."

"The sex act is built entirely on faith, dear sir. A faith that the coupling will even get started, in the first place. Then there's the expectation naked bodies will fit. And that the ultimate is going to please the co-dependents—like that? Hirsch?— and what good is your God-given free-thinking if you waste it on imaginary things like a pope who only fakes charity? You and I should start a business and manufacture something. How 'bout, let's see, how 'bout a combination bed and cash register? Bang!" She pauses.

All the room's heroes are mute. Her eyes suddenly go to Stone whose lips are moving to some semblance of *boptitude*. "Stoners, man!' she exults. "Your paramour is your piano. You'd kiss that keyboard if it could love you back, yeah? Speaking of which, unleash the beast and let's do a tune. I know one that you wrote long ago, eh? I sing, You play."

Stone is plotzed with disbelief. His face slowly slips into a blank mask. He struggles to speak. "Where where.... I mean, you got my lyrics, my lilacs? my poppy-petalled speculations, man? and the rain, you dig, spattering its words?"

"Come on, Stonaroony." She mock-helps him over to the piano, flashes a volcanic smile at the gathering, She faces the room and, immediately sings the first line of what is Stone's own published composition.

"Whenever life gets special..."

*(Stone chimes in some notes
behind her, exactly in the key she began in.)*

This all-too-weak flesh'll
Give way to passion.

So I fell in love quite blindly
Asking only that he treat me kindly

As is the faaaashun.

(Stone slowly cascades a chord progression and waits for her.)

"Just what I wanted
The loss of you.

Just what I wanted
I can't pursue.

No need at all to love him any longer.
Heaven knows I should have been much stronger.

I know they're saying, now that our romance is through
'What was the name of...',
They'll make a game of
forgetting you know who.

My loneliness showing,
everyone knowing
that just what I wanted
somehow can't come true."

The emotion of the end-lyrics warms its way into her eyes and her lips as she portrays the loneliness of the torch singer.

(A glissando re-ignites the melody's fading moments for an encore of the final sentiment)

No mistletoe-ing
(she pauses)

I won't be goooo-ing

'Cause just what I wanted

somehow can't come true."

The listeners sit stunned. They've never heard it. And not sure the song's over. I very lightly clap/ summon their applause which intensifies into a roaring sexual ovation. And then a fresh outburst from the piano kicks up a bright, accelerando as intro to another Stone composition.

For the moment, Doll retains her affected pose but on one hand her fingers are snapping to the new beat. She raises her head and her face is now a wicked, knowing *moue*. She raises an arm to point and sweep across the company as she sings:

I'm gonna kick the dust from my heels
Squeeze this old world to see how it feels.

I'll do my hitch in the show for the run of it.
I'll be a bitch. . .or maybe the son of it (the fun of it)

I'm gonna drink as much as I please
Won't wear a dress that covers my kneeeees.

But there is one thing, baby, that I'll never do:
That's fall again

for someone like you.

(*Piano solo reprising the next chorus as Stone lays down the block chords of George Shearing stylings*)

During this obbligato, Doll kicks off the sling-pumps and vamps about the seated guests, keeping her arms stretched high above, snapping her fingers in ravishment and tossing the coif and shaking the hips for all the world. Men's eyes are glazed, drinks inert and unremembered in their hands.

Now the arms reach out to either side as she frisks her way back to the piano in perfect collaboration with the precise, vocal moment of the second chorus.

"I'm tokin' til I'm high as the moon
Get Stone to help me carry a tune

I'll get a man who never finds faults with me
Lookin' for someone somewhere somehow to waltz with me (one-two-three)

So sweetie darling baby hooray
Bette Midler look out maybe I'm gay

It's all so hot and crazy but I know it's true

I'll never risk a kiss
The kind I'd really miss

on someone　　　　liiiiiiiike　　　　youuuuuu."

The crowd goes wild is all I can think. Except Hirsch, they are standing, applauding, whistling. Doll does a few hand-over-the-heart curtsies and then a grand gesture to Stone who is going wildly extempore on the melody. Now she folds hands prayer-like and bows. Another salute to Stone who finally looks up in acknowledgement as he holds down the pedal and trills a final, huge, flatted-fifth chord.

XVI

This   **Mother of God**
    is what's   **you sing like** *you*
      wonderful   an angel
      your   **you're**   *boogie,*
      room   **so**   *girl*
      number   **very**

                talented and, you know, a great idea would be for all of us to provide some of our poetry we're doing tonight so Stone could consult his piano and set our lyrics to his own, created music. Whaddaythink? Hirsch? You too." This is the enthusing Millie.

With Stone still softly jamming, Hirsch abruptly hurls herself from her chair and into a fairly-decent rendition of The Charleston, slightly bent over, moving her arms in time with her rapid, repeating steps and her mouth a curve of determination.

"You *are* evil," twits Freeman.

Doll likes Hirsch's act. "Dance dance dance. C'mon, team! Let 'er move!"

Stone segues into "Fats" Waller, stride-piano mode, left hand playing ump-chuck, and simple octaves driving the melody.

Soon she tires. Modigliani seeps back into her features, and Stone ends the improvisation. Cheers and applause for her tour de *farce*. She puts hand to chest in mock-modesty.

Host goes over to bow and then kisses her hand. "Hirsch, your dance style is so American. Where's all that Austrian influence, if you don't mind my asking? I actually enjoy the legacy of your *Volksmusik*. All those zithers and harmonicas and the yodeling from the alpine farmers as they hurl themselves at their listeners."

Her face has a fixed look to it.

He claps his personal, brief ovation, then announces: "Well! That was quite a novelty, my dears. But, say! What did our Millie come up with moments ago? Another capital idea, everyone! Our poems, our verses. Melded into music. Stone here can turn 'em all into song for us, can't you, Stone? He has the entire night all to himself. It will be a new artform to bring us to the end of writers' enslavement." His face is now resplendent with the grand assumption that those in the room can live a better life. He raises his drink to me. "And maybe Storey here will provide a few lines also for us. Some light verse perhaps. Of course, you'll contibute."

"Dramaturgy scripturgy metalurgy," grumbles Stone.

"The old master hated mobs, too. *Mobile vulgus*," chimes in Host.

Millie stands up. "Small-town Billy Shakespeare leaves Stratford, goes to London to become an actor and suddenly starts writing masterpieces." She counts on her fingers all the human issues...... debauchery......plotters......assassins...... roaming swordsmen. Ahyes? So how could a provincial actor gain such an intimate knowledge of court life? How about all his Italian stuff and he never traveled there? He stays disguised behind his skills and inspires us to be jealous. *Merde*!" she sighs. "People prefer mysteries to answers anyway. Don't they."

"Our divine William re-wrote the works of other dramatists," say I. "There isn't even a record that he attended grammar school either, you know.

Host is the honest academic on such things. "Ah, but so worthy a fellow was our Shakespeare. I am prompted by a famous memorial from Jonson— poet laureate, no less—in which he calls this author the 'Sweet swan of Avon.' Moreover, the curriculum of an Elizabethan school back then had a strong, classical history and literary bias. As the son of a leading Stratford citizen, our bard would have been entitled to a free education. There are no records of any of the pupils at Stratford grammar school until a century later."

How promising is this realm of classical discourse. "Ben Jonson did not attend university either," I offer. "Yet he went on to great reknown for his learning. I do take more issue with some of the silly, bard plot-lines. A real Lord Capulet would never have involved himself with domestic wedding details in the way Juliet's father does. 'Let's hang around for a bit,' Macbeth might have told his worked-up wife. 'Wait and see what comes along. We don't need to start murdering everybody in the cast just to get a quick upgrading'."

"Jolly good," comes the landlord.

"And Hamlet?" I continue. "Back to school for you and take your two weird friends with you. Because no one ever pleases his father. In this case, even after he's gone. And while you're studying, figure out why you dumped that cutie-pie Ophelia. She loved your poetry. You break her heart, and her sanity goes with it. What?! So you'll be king someday, and all you'll get is a bigger castle?"

"Hear hear!" "Keep going! "Bravo!" "Groovy as a movie!" "Who else?"

"Othello, too. The Moor has a great wife. Then he's a General on the battlefield but a raw recruit in the boudoir. It's natural for newlyweds to quarrel especially when the bride is so young. She's in bed half the play. What more does he want? In marriage, you make what you can of love. A lesson in romantic pride? Or was he actually just hot for that Iago bastard?"

"Marriage is a dance through money." It's Hirsch.

"'Shall I compare thee to a summer's day....'" Freeman trying something Shakespearean.

Millie: "Shakespeare's tyrants move beyond Machiavelli. I mean, it's the life dedicated to power that really calls for a distortion of human nature. It's called evil."

The ultimate evil is death, I'm thinking. But the priest will be heard.

"Let me say that good and evil are not just values," he begins. "Good means life and evil is death. It's all in Deuteronomy 30. Evil means the other guy. Somebody else is evil. YOU are nefarious. I am good. YOU are a villain. I am an innocent. You are the Frankenstein." He nods his head in self-appraisal. "How do humans become rendered into evil things? we may ask. It all starts with all of us together concentrated on building enemies. The tools for such connivance come to us in—let's see—we establish our enemy camps by using courtrooms, schoolhouses, pulpits, altars, conglomerates, politics, automobile traffic, the post office, crowded theaters, sports and the media." The curate is on his way to glory. "We're only united in this country when we're against something. Can we struggle effectively against evil without becoming tainted ourselves when I first began delving into the subject of evil... economists consider enemies to be hedonisstic

competitors for scarce resources..." **God. I
have to go to the bathroom. It's damn Shakespeare
and now evil. Am I the only one with kidneys?** *"...I
believed in evil as original sin as built into
our natures evil should be fought by another
kind of evil..."* **Ohlord. Wherethehell'sthepotty!
I must whisper. "Um, Host. I need the men's for a
mo."**

**"Through there," he's pointing, "and right first
door."**

XVII

I'm on my way. Priest continues on his. *"...evil
grows from the quest to defeat the..."* **I close
the door behind me and enter a cluttered workroom
with a** *melange* **of art renderings crowding its entire
wallspace. I spy the man's computer in the corner
but duty calls as I open the door to the BR. OHboy.
Toilet seat up, zipper down and deliverance at last.
Not from evil, either. The relieving stream is clear
and sustained. Jesus! The exact, same maleness
either pours away the body waste or it shoots out
new life. What irony. Still going tinkle. So where
have I gotten myself. This unshackled, literary
daring may be just monstrous folly or it seems
I've stopped writing, too, really. I'm done peeing.
Hands. MIrror. Where's a towel? Writers are all
drowning, trying to tell a story that's lying there like
an empty tooth paste tube. The hope that a blank
page will have its expectation alleviated. Soon then
the consequences of ink will end the stand-off.
Such admirable nonsense. Am I really that 80-year-
old, flaunty ghost in the looking glass? Hostage**

to my creations now. Players, host, author and Pirandello alike swept in tandem toward our last portion. What serene and spacious despair! Almost homosexual in its sense of companionship. I smile a ridiculous affectation at my reflection and work into a left-handed look in order to come out with a soft-pitched, essy voice: "I just can't help looking gay," I say loudly to my despairing reflection. "I put on a little gown and everybody says, 'Who's the homo in the dress'?"

At this moment of tricked-up camp, as if timed by some theatrical director, Freeman is abruptly just entering the BR. Hearing my aging-queen refrain, he's right there with his own nellie-voice concoction, "Now I know why gay men have no second dates," he declares and goes right to the toidey as if he too were the only one currently in the room.

Then he comes to the mirror. "You know, when I do a gay bit in my act, I go: "I feel like Norma Desmond." as he exaggerates the 's'. He stares another moment of self-mockery. "Do I look too wrinkled? No, no, not my suit, my face." He pulls back his cheeks toward his ears and says, "Let's find better lighting." He laughs a throaty Tallulah Bankhead aw-haw-haw, and I am losing it he is so the exquisite drag-hussy for the moment's mimicking.

I return to my actual self: "I can't undertstand why gay people want to be in the military…because they only get one outfit to wear."

"And there's such a thing as the gay mafia," he counters. "If you cross them, they will come to your apartment and break the legs on your coffee table."

We're washing our hands and looking for proper towels. Only tiny, paper, doily ones are provided.

"No real towels! Godamn these horrible, non-drying cruddies, right?"

I know what he means. "I gotta tell you," I say. "The time in New York I unadvisedly entered a certain bar down in the East Village in order to hit the jon right away real quick. The name of the place was 'The Duchess'. Big clue that I never picked up on. The doorman tried to stall me from coming in but when ya gotta go, but anyway It was all the way to the back and as I'm moving along through the place I realize from the stares and really bad vibes from a million female customers on my way through that I was one solo, major-unwelcome male but I could not wait or care under the circumstances and finally got myself to the singular rest-room as there WAS no men's room and two gals were primping in there and all I could do was get to the toilet in one of the stalls, finish up and repeat the long walk the hell out of there. The doorman was still laughing. Who wouldn't want to be a tackle on a girl's football team, though, eh?"

We move out and into Host's workroom , and I can sense Freeman doesn't want to join the others just yet. We sit.

"Storey. You got a great nickname. Should be mine. Every joke's a story. I'm just the one telling them. It's me being a slave of some internal power that must make people laugh. Because I am driven to be loved by everyone. From afar, of course. That fricking, hostile, critical mass of humanity that exists on the other side of the footlights or the microphone! Why suppose that people like me want to do jokes? Being funny is the same as music. You got to have tension. Here's a set-up. Guy and his wife go to a doctor. She needs a flu shot. She hates, absolutely hates the idea of an injection, a piece of metal going into her flesh. The husband is calming her down before the doctor comes in. The nurse sees what's going on. She says, 'Madam, don't worry about the injection, it'll just be a little prick with a needle' and the wife says, 'I know what he is but I still don't like it'."

We both laugh this man is so likeable one of those guys who has a kind of embarrassed chuckle of his own to get you started and I say, "I think of Milton Berle's great line when he says to somebody in the audience 'I remember you heckling me 20 years ago I never forget a suit' and Freeman does, there's this Catholic girl she goes to confession she says she has to alleviate her soul and she tells the priest, 'Father, I can't help myself. I want to hold men down. I want to whip them. I want to force them to caress my body' and the priest tells her, 'Take your time, say ten Hail Marys and meet me in a couple minutes behind the Exxon station' and mine is "It's Passover and a Jewish guy is eating his lunch in the park a blind man sits down next to him so the Jewish guy offers him some of his lunch a piece of matzos the blind man takes it, fingers it a moment and says who writes this crap' Freeman likes it and his is you want a Jewish joke

Jewish guy is walking on the beach and he sees a lamp washed up on shore so he picks it up rubs it and a genie appears and says 'you got one wish' so the Jewish guy pulls a map out of his pocket and says 'this is a map of the Middle East and points and says 'here is Israel completely surrounded by hostile countries and they're always fighting and killing and my wish is that there would be absolute peace in the Middle East' and the genie says 'hey hey, that's much too big an order even for me only God knows why there is such violence going on and how to end it' and so 'all right, says the Jew, here's another one then I have been married to the same Jewish woman for 20 years and in all that time she has never once given me a blow-job' the genie thinks a few seconds and gives a deep sigh and then says 'lemme see that map again' and my turn is did you hear about the guy at the dentist for oral surgery and the dentist mentions novacaine and the patient says 'novacaine hurts too much' and so the dentist suggests gas and the guy says he doesn't trust being unconscious and the dentist hands him a Viagra pill and the guy says 'what's that for?' and the dentist says 'so when the pain starts you'll have something to hold onto'."

We are having too much fun laughing like hell as Doll enters from the main room. She puts on a huge, reprimanding smirk. "Well. Seigfried and Roy." She strolls toward the BR as she remarks over her shoulder, "How are YOU two getting along?" She leaves the door from the main room ajar. "There is something a woman never ever does," say I, "and that is shut the door tightly when she leaves a room and it's because her damnable, unhealable intuition for nebshit intrusion means she wants men to sense that she is somehow still present. There. How's that?"

We both watch her disappear. We look at each other. "It's the voice that determines the woman," Freeman announces, as if Doll's entire value were endangered by her frivolous speech.

"Beauty's only a light-swtich away," I say.

He goes, "A hooker once told me she had a headache," .

Me: "The doctor calls Mrs. Cohen and tells her, 'Mrs. Cohen. Your check came back.' And she says, 'So did my arthritis'."

We are grinning at each other with that shared fast-humor hipness.

Him: "Freud said penis envy meant that every woman wanted a penis. And Yung thought that every woman......" I join him in announcing the punch line, "......wanted *his* penis." And Doll is talking as she enters from the bathroom.

"While you two perverts were in the potty and draining the monsters, I had a nice chat with Hirsch and, you know, Freeman, you're not the villain she makes you out to be. You're just a philandering prick like every other man."

He answers, "Hey, if yer gonna regret this in the mornin', we can sleep til noon."

He is still sitting. She moves directly to him. "All blondes are not dumb," she says. "But all men are men." She sticks out a tiny tongue, wiggles it. Now she spots me. Takes a deep breath, holds it. Then: "No one can make you feel inferior without your consent......Eleanor Roosevelt!"

I try: "Taking you in is like eating an entire box of chocolate liqueurs in one go......Truman Capote! Sort of."

"Personally," offers Freeman, "I can never be cured of anything without plenty of alcohol and women......Rich Freeman!"

She sinks down upon a hassock, her bearing somehow completely devoid of ostentation. "My agenda, gentlemen, is to look good while doing bad. I am lights, camera but not necessarily action. I tell all men, don't paint your bridges with blood if you're going to burn them." She slits her eyes and puts on a new, mysterious beauty.

Freeman gets up slowly, takes her hand to kiss it. Then, in a warm voice, "I'm all about chivalry."

I offer my inspired suggestion: "Thank goodness we all drink the same language," which is squandered on these two who are playing the only game there is for them: lying.

"You know, baby Doll darling." He's on big now. "My mom is 93 years old and I went out to see her the other day and I made a terrible Freudian slip. We were eating one of her usual dinners and what

I meant to say was, 'Pass the salt but what I said was, 'You bitch, you ruined my life'."

I am exploding. She is countering, "Well, you know, when I was a waitress, some killer party-man gave me twenty dollars for a tip and came on with his big, bullshit grin and says, 'See all this big money, and now your grandmother can have that operation', and I gave him back the 2 ten-spots and told him, 'Don't bother, she decided she still wants to be a woman'."

He's: "Then how about you and me and a little foreplay?"

And she's: "Foreplay? Sounds like golf. First you holler 'Fore' and then you play. Right?

I try: "At least in tennis, there's love."

"Going to bed with a woman is great stuff," he says. "Staying up all night looking for one is what does me in."

She: "So that's why your fly is always open."

And I: "The dead bird does not leave the nest."

"Well!" says Freeman. "That was a quick line."

"Churchill," say I.

And I am buoying Doll to her feet. She favors me with her lavish, foxy-best look and then, as she crosses to the door, "Golf is the slowest game in the world. Driving something into a hole." She turns back for a gratuitous exit line, "The fastest game in the world......is when it slips out." Bam-gone.

How long do we two guys stare at the door? It has been left wide open. Now we see Hirsch on her way to us.

"Uh-oh. I'm not here anymore," says Freeman. "Talking to her is like taking a lion for a walk."

He gives way as she enters the room. "And now, ladies and gentlemen," he announces. "May I introduce the renowned inventor of endlessness, Hirrrrrrrrrsh Freeeeee-munnnnnnnn!" He mock applauds a few seconds and bows out the door.

Here the lady is. Somehow she has found a long scarf which is tied loosely about her neck and hanging below her thin waist. Her body imitates a Modiglianisculpturegivenevenmoreverisimulitude as the artist was known to have stolen stone from building sites. She does a light tap-dance across and into the bathroom. I go over and close the other door. I'm alone now to ponder.

So Hirsch is Javert to Freeman's Valjean. She the obsessive pursuer who continuously hunts, tracks down and still loses her quarry. And I am Victor Hugo without Schonberg and Kretz, the '*Les Miz*' guys. Ah, that most admirable nonsense which is the will to write. Seven per-cent of us are doomed to be authors and we will be afflicted by this awful mentality that Styron described as a gray drizzle of horror...a storm of murk. For me, a blank page must have its expectations alleviated. Ink be thy destiny. "Who am I?" utters playwright Pirandello. His characters have a source of tragedy with their search for an inspired end to their unresolved drama. . These fictional personages now more authentic than real ones. They need an author. Those in the title are called into existence by the playwright who soon deserts them. But a created personality will never die. A man will die. The writer, the instrument of creation is mortal but what he has summoned and assembled will never die. Whoever has the luck to be born in a writer's mind can laugh at death. A fictional figure has a permanence that comes from an unchanging text. Pirandello once said, "I am a child of chaos."

What of my six darlings, stuck with them as I am in this traveling geometry! I once thought up something called Booklovers' Block where people borrow too many books out of the library and then get into a panic because they haven't read more than a few pages of each one and the due date is near and the penalties will be a terrible psychological onus to them. And they are so confounded and inhibited that the very act of reading is stifled. They are the same readers who go to used-book shops or to stores with stacked publications that are on discount outside the premises or those libraries that have book sales and these people buy a Conrad or Moby Dick because they've never read them and it would be important at last to check out a masterpiece or two and realize somehow what the hell pursuing a white whale is all about. But this kind of fortune-cookie reading means deserting the computer and sitting down somewhere without the TV on and actually dip into a classic. Right.

XVIII

A distant toilet flushes. I can assume that Hirsch, the untamed shrew of Freeman's existence is soon to be standing here explaining herself.

Indeed, now she enters, "That's where a husband comes in," she sighs. "When his solutions bring new problems." Thus said as if she and I are simply now continuing an already-started conversation about him.

"My husband has a putrified vision of women. He just can't turn off that pussy-radar of his. Mind if I join you?" She sits apparently by intuition in his previously occupied chair. "I always tell him that if it's a boring party, just leave it that way." She likes this. "You know, Storey, is that your name, how appropriate right? It's so off-hand as you are here listening to our storrrrries because nobody's supposed to write anything anymore except for yours truly and I'm the one who can't write because when I try I'm losing my verbs. First the nouns and after that the verbs. Where was I?"

"You were talking about...."

"Yes, now I got it. I once went to a Halloween party as HIM. Because he needs to realize what he does to other people all the time. I know him and he doesn't accept it. He needs to offend people, too. So. There is the point. It's him. My closest friends I have, they know what I must submit to. My Aunt Celia always said about the good the very goodness in me. I have crossed the street to pick up after someone. There must be a choice. I find it. I stay."

"But how did the party go?"

"What?"

"The Halloween thing?"

"I can't remember much that I did. Why would you want masqueraded people to behave like themselves? I can tell you though, it is both maddening AND flattering to be feeling replaced and at the same time seen as being something new. My husband cast me, put me in some of his amateur plays, y'know, due to that I was a quick study. He seemed surprised. The other actors did well with me in my part. My potentials were always liked. But they were people on a stage with me. They were anticipating and ready to react to every single thing I said in my role. You feel like you have just awoken for the first time despite whatever has happened. You have to affirm your existence."

"Did he ever say he loved you?"

"You can't say you love me until you know what hurts me." She squints grimly. "Do you know my therapist says I also have prosopopoeia."

"Migawd! What's that!"

"That's, um, where a person absent or dead is represented as speaking."

"Your shrink gives you a lot to carry around with you.

She gets up and walks about, displaying her thinny-thin bearing. "I'm not paranoid. Somebody out to get me has got me already. Freezerman. The time in therapy is just a place. I need my nice bed. Covers. Warm. Tomorrow. I will lie down and the doctors aren't there. This room is cold."

She unties the huge scarf and places it about her torso. "The night I did sex with my husband before I married him it was a cheap room the Fort Pitt Hotel in Pittsburgh. I bathed in the tub for awhile first. Let him wait. I was damn good-looking and a dancer, too. Recovering codependents at Auddico all clapped hands when I sent him the divorce papers. I didn't want to leave him but the applause. Jesus Christ! The approval! From all those people at the meetings! Their cheers were the highest point in my life."

She stops pacing and turns to me. "Nothing is happening to me today."

"I was going to say about your sense of being an actress. Your temperament endows you perfectly to Shakespeare. He has all these powerful, restive, ambitious women who are willing to take extreme risks even if they have to distort everything. You're right up there with the fictional goddesses of the theater.

"I can't write. What am I doing in a novel about writers?"

What did she just say!?

"Are you speculating that you're living someone's novel?"

"Am I?" Her expression slowly fills with discovery, "Maybe I mean it's novel, a novel thing. To be in custody with people with whom I share nothing essential."

"Maybe you mean it's the elegant illusion that we live another life?"

She whirls her scarf away, knots it bizarrely around the neck and poses a hand on her hip. It's one of Lear's nasty daughters. She could do it. "I see, dear Storey-teller, that I've got you wondering what it is I know. First of all, you are somehow tied to the six of us I'm not counting Host but you are the co-dependent around here. You need this crowd for some motive and take it from a professional co-dependent my brain's in on it, too."

"You know it seems both of us are obsessives. And here we are in the midst of people trying to stop their compulsions." I venture a smile.

"So what are you stirring up here, Mister Storman sir? I sincerely doubt that Host is telling the truth about your presence. Indeed, you are a writer. You talk like a writer. You look like one and you dress like one. And, and, your authors in the next room, now how or why would anyone care to stop others from their sacred calling? Can't you see it? I want to think and people won't let me. My mind gives way the brain loses control I don't seem to be anybody anymore."

"I'm sorry you sense that you're so all alone as if stuck in present tense."

"Don't pretend to be sorry. Pretend to be concerned. That's how I always like Virginia Woolf."

"Yes, all that floating sensibility but no fixed characters."

"Virginia deals with each moment. The thought and the sensation. The voice of the sea. I often feel as if I am standing in water just up to my nose. Inclusion of things I don't belong in."

"Yes, but if you surrender to the water, it buoys you up. It's like keeping on with the swimming, not just staying still."

Her expression slowly fills with discovery and the eyes determined to provoke something in me. "Writing a novel is a ludicrous way to die, wouldn't you say?" She does signal some possible clairvoyance into my Pirandellan journalizing. "Can people in fiction be more actual than real people? Huh?" Now her lids close in some kind of faux-Zen, unnatural breathing thing. An abstract, mystical, sightless appearance. Also, her scarf is now hooding her self. Her persona somehow makes me think of that Grim Reaper guy who appears in cartoons or Grand Gingnol or at any chance to alarm someone as if each and every death were to arrive in this theatrical way. She slowly languishes to the floor and continues her Buddhist inspiration. "Virginia," she intones.

I do remember Virginia Woolf. And water. In "The Waves" she comes on writing about six characters. Think of that! Six! Whoa! And each of these Woolf characters is distinct, yet together they compose a gestalt, and in my gang, this would mean the dreaded scripturgia addiction. One of the personalities in that Woolf novel I think she called it a play-poem was a Rhonda or a Rhoda she's riddled with self-doubt and anxiety which sounds exactly like the quarrelsome Hirsch, always rejecting and indicting any kind of human compromise, always seeking out solitude. As my *amiga* settles herself there in abstraction, I wish I could be sure of what she's been talking about. Now this person is spellbound, I should wait till she's over it all and meantime intuit a way out of continuing too long in someone else's possibilities. She sits in silence. No change. Peace. Or just privacy? I am dying for a drink.

XIX

As I move to slip out politely for the main room, "Stay!" is the only thing I am able to say to her, and why do I think doggie-talk will help. I've got Virginia Woolf's six to add to Luigi PIrandello's six to add to my own six! And it's Hirsch telling me about "The Waves" and she fears she's drowning (!). Somehow she's making me see the concurrency of it all.

I enter to the sound of Millie discoursing, *"...but he kept me in cooks, chauffeurs, paintings, beautiful clothes and as long as I was going to be a writer..."*

They all come on as I appear: "There he is! Hail the conquering author! He's the only one's allowed."

I'm: "How nice of you all to give me this welcome and where are the cannons please?"

"How many n's in that?" Father P with this.

I go to shake the witty man's hand. I see Stone is absent. So is Doll. Can 'maryjane' be far behind?

"You're missing the magnificent Millie going over her list of husbands," Host says. "Many of them her own."

She holds an empty champagne goblet, a half-spent bottle pushed down in its ice-bucket. "I have been a kind of flesh-and-blood *trompe l'oeil* to certain spoiled men. Their inner eye expects some heavenly arrangement that would merge our two financial statements. I married only one of them and he died choking on a piece of crayfish wasn't even lobster and I now survive knowing that those who have money are wise. And good-looking. And can sing well also."

She taps the glass with her fingernail but as Host rises, she holds it out for a splash of the sidecar cocktail. She goes right on. "It's no sense being pointlessly rich unless you are a liberal." She quick-glance appraises all present and, "By a liberal, they mean someone who looks ahead and not behind, someone who welcomes new ideas without being one of those rigid reactionaries, someone who cares about the welfare of the people, their health, their schools, their liberties. On the other hand, liberals are far too busy evaluating failure."

She takes just a sip. "Republican leadership is irresponsibly cheering on the thuggish crowds. Why should we insist on rewriting history just to make people feel good? That's not history, anyway.

More like psychiatry." She raises both hands in complete self-satisfaction at the wordplay.

I am feeling reasonably implicated now. "It's the Bush people who gave us wars being fought for the improvement of foreigners," I opine. "And the minute we started looking for terrorists in Iraq, we became terrorists."

"A Roman historian Tacitus declared, 'The enemy-invader creates a desolation of the soul and calls it peace'," intones the good priest.

"Well, Father," goes Millie, "I say Christianity as an institution can solve the calamitous mistake of the Middle East. The power of the Vatican and, more so, the invincible American Catholics could offer their Jesus ornaments of peace and understanding to their Islam brothers. They could set up a dialogue, take on the cause of the insurgents, open their wallets and show what Christianity can really bring off. But they are just not going to. Seems they're stuck in their version of the GOP. Just say no way. They are only interested in preserving their control over their constituents through fund-raising."

"The fundamental task of a religion is to serve God," priest announces. "The church is not a branch of a political party. . .it's mission must be everlastingly identified. Once Christians give themselves away to influence-peddling, they cease to be a church. That decision makes them nothing more than a branch office of the GOP's factional expedient. In this case, the First Republican Church of America. Using the ministry for some politician and shouting from the pulpit about who should get voted in keeps things far from Jesus. They are getting their values from somewhere else. Not from our lord." He is smiling now. "I shouldn't get into preaching like this. Somehow religion outside the church gets to be annoying."

A sense of idleness briefly takes over their mood. What a helping of humanity is a group of people in collaborative stillness, abstracted as if lost in a masterpiece! Sometimes a truth can exist by its own majesty. And its mysterious language is stillness. I think of Mother Teresa's precious quote, 'God is the friend of silence.' She was consecrated to be purely at home with the way nature grows in quietude, to see all of the heavenly extraterrestrials and how they move in tranquility. The deaf know this world where there is no noise and no restlessness, no tone_of meaning, and all in modesty. The mime Marceau wrote that "Music and silence combine strongly because silence is full of music." We writers compose with only the voiceless representations of the mind to shape our thoughts. Advocates of contemplation, we are at war with words to conquer them and force out their beauty. Sometimes they reward us with eudaemonia."

I can hear Stone in full-throated conversation with Doll as they burst through the outside back-door, ",,,,*but I got to toss my dreams so* that all the people will disappear and then the soul **can hum its existence night after……okay…hey!**" He is indifferent to the stares of the assemblage. "**Dudes still tryin' to sell sanity?**" as he waves off the imperturbable Host who is raising the cocktail shaker to him for sampling. "**Jazz is just art with a bag of weed tied** to its collar. Host-man. That's what 'Trane said. And if anybody wants a hit of my kind of jewelry you know the one that loves you back merrywanna always makes me want to dig Bartok you know like the second concerto that cat was way into zen sounds, y'all………"

"ZEN IS……" This is Doll actually managing a shouted interruption. She smiles a frozen portrayal as her point is completely muddled. She seems to want to recover but her eyes don't. "Zen! Zen is actually I mean really it is like mental nudism only you can keep your clothes on all the time that's it."

"Zen is just endless sabbath," offers the priest. "Without worship, though."

She curtsies, a forefinger to her chin. "Your holiness." She whirls about and comes out with, "Now Stone. Stone is going to jazz-rape the piano, aren't you , maestro? The keyboard is there to be beaten and invaded and conquered and it will not rest until each of you all will share in…." She again cannot find a single, mental souvenir to put into words. "I swoon," she goes. Back of hand now to her forehead.

The priest lets go an unusally loud hiccup. "Huptt," is the sound it makes.

Doll eyes him, ready with rescue, "Now, Father. Father, the hiccups will go away if you will just listen to me and now now I want you to take a deep breath and hold it as long as ('huptt') oh-oh, okay, start again."

"Thank you, dear girl. I'm off to the rest-room." He heads to the BR as he murmurs, "....who doesn't prefer fiction to reality. Huptt! Oh. Excuse me, Hirsch." His bulk disappears. Door is closed on those two.

Freeman is heard: "So what is this, a convention of stoics? Nietzsche got bigger laughs when he played the Vatican. Should we all stop drinking? Hello? I think we're moving away from our destinies here. How 'bout it, Storey? You just spent an eternity in the next room listening to Hirsch so you ought to be desperate to hear the sound of your own voice. She hangs out with that bad crowd inside her head, or didn't I already say that?"

As he speaks, I don't know if I should defend her in that I don't understand her. She is the one right out of V. Woolf who has failed to meet the others on the common ground of cosmic continuity. All this as she slaves through the deterioration of her marital conditions, gradually slipping into what V called the automatic, customary, unconscious days on either side. Freeman now doing Edward G. Robinson: "So you won't talk, eh? All right, I gotta gat, see?! How about Cagney? he says: "Youah the guyee that killed my brothah! Gable?: Frankly, my dear, I don't give a damn."

Doll is hysterical. I applaud. He is dead on. And still on: "Hey. How about the guy gettin' a haircut and he hears a fire siren and tells the barber I got to go now and the barber says, oh, you're a fireman and the guy says, no, my girlfriend's husband is."

All look about at each other as if expecting a single voice to carry on. Stone is at the piano, head down and staring at the keys. Host is in his stuffed chair. Millie examines her diamond rings. Doll is firing up a J and Freeman's eyes are hot on me (I'm all he's got): "So what luck did you have with Medusa?" he goes. "You didn't stare into her eyes, did you?"

And I: "Too bad she can't turn Stone into a man."

"Ewww. Terrible," says Host at the pun. "But we were going to put some poetry into song by way of Mr. Stone. I assume Alec Templeton over there at the keyboard has a million melodies at the ready. Is there anybody here's got verses primed for instant fame? Anything ridiculous that we can recite for right now. Just to have us a warm-up. Whatever rubbish that might be stored in your memories will do quite nicely."

They each begin to take up the task of coming up with any favorite, ancient doggerel, which calls for either pacing or sitting with closed eyes, lips moving, thinking of their bygone bouquets of mirth or love or loss, Stone the only one a lanky frame poised as a contemplative gargoyle over his upcoming, overnight, keyboard scourings.

Will these lines be their personal creations or just echoes of my own through their imaginations? I have a sudden, oceanic feeling of anxiety. How much acceptance do I really want here? What god am I? The judgmental creator or the protecting architect? Don't my sexy sixies have a communal doubt? Do they all share the uncertainty whether they are able to stay unequivocally 'dry' much longer?

Host has given up the barrage of cocktails and comes over to confer. He softens his voice. "Don't trouble your head by pitching in with this dodgy bunch. Most of them aren't a patch on your own poetry." How does he suppose this!

"I would think, Host, that you would try to wean these former writers by at least allocating them into short stories. Melville, Hawthorne and James come to mind."

"Good ones! But too late for that, you see. It's Stone now to drive them into another art. Lyricism."

"But how. . ."

"Ah, dear boy. It's time for the practice poetry. Do slip into the other room and fetch Hirsch and Father so they can throw in with this lot. Yes." He turns his face in slight hesitation as if ready with an exquisite thing to say. He comes out with: "Experience as opposed to philosophy," His hushed tone aspires to an undeserved attention. "All the unique irrepeatability is opposed to philosophy which turns out to be too generalized." His face is close as his whisper. "Universality." He waits and inhales softly as if to extract from me any sense of concurrence."

XX

My brain goes, "Where's the drink? Where's the al co hol?" And suddenly, I remember planning to refresh Hirsch anyway. I dip away from my dear gentleman and coast past the oaken table, swoop up a carafe of sidecars and pour the entire mix—the libation and my fugitive self and my expectations—into the next-door scene of priest and she-wolf.

There sits bless-me father softly, theatrically snoring away and Hirsch still in Zen's zenith, paradoxically on the floor.

"Why don't we two find a noose we can share?" I intentionally say quite loudly to her.

She opens one eye. "And who shall be the hangman?"

I hopefully offer her a hand up. "We all love martyrdom. Even though not terribly churchy about it."

She suddenly bounds to her feet as adroitly as a gymnast. "Thunderstorms, waves and waterfalls are the cause of negative ions. That's the deal regarding me and water. So we can sit. There's a very distracting motive in your makeup that seems to get the picture about me. Like my god-damn empire of depression which really doesn't send out clear signals for others to catch onto. A stranger everywhere, even to myself. I am supposed to stay silent within the pristine moment. That's what they say to me at Auddico. That's Authors coAddicted for the suffering wives." She eyes the priest. "You know? The world's just a planet called THEM."

I grab two glasses out of their holders and pour us some cocktail.

Somehow she's refreshed. And now in a chair. Raises the drink to her nose for a sniff and immediately puts it down nearby.

"How was your Zenimation?" I put it.

"I saw you as a writer, you know," she charges. "You were sitting in a sunny backyard and putting some thoughts together with classical music it was Mahler and do you mind if I finish. . ."

"I'm not interrupting you."

"And on a nearby, imaginary lake, it was me aboard a sailboat. And you know how this ship doesn't flop over?"

"The vessel stays its balance. The, uh, lead hull commands uprightness as the wind strikes the sail."

"And there you have it. You don't talk like other people. That's the clue as to your identity."

"What's the clue to yours?"

"Zen's where I get all my low-down. Never try to turn the moment into yesterday. You have to personally seep into everything, you know? Nothing is permanent. Nothing is everything. How's that?"

"Well, isn't Zen being stripped down of everything and being placed into a raw environment where you're thrown upon yourself?"

"Yeah yeah so yeah so anyway the part that is tough for me is that NOW has to be enough. But then look just now is gone now. And then now is new. And I can't get over being separate and whole at the same time. So I gave up all my dramatic stories about the past. How different the world becomes then."

She stops to scowl at me in complete dissatisfaction. Takes up the drink and gulps a huge swallow without looking away from my eyes. "I am a chronophile also. It's like someone who stares all day at a broken clock. You know what I mean we all wake up and immediately want to know what time it is on any given day? Well, there's a digital clock right there in my bedroom. I feel I have just woken up for the first time despite whatever has happened calculating to guarantee my existence. It's like I can't find where I was in a book I'm reading. I am thrown back again into the abyss of anywhere at all. There is a useless future for each moment gone :: with every tick of the clock. My shrink says to practice letting things be. But how can I when there are, um, non-causal links of coincidence. What's that called, uhhh…"

"Synchronicity," slowly utters the priest. . .his eyes stay closed.

She points her tiny lips. "Synchronicity. That's when two things happen at the same time and…."

"Temporary coincidental occurrences. Thus synchronicity." the priest has joined in, now wide awake.

Hlrsch: "Yeah. Here's my sink-thing. This is good. My therapist says the best way to deal with addiction is to take up another one. Pretty soon you have too many and they all push everything out isn't that true so I started with the displays on digital clocks. It was a bright, cold day in April and the clocks were striking their obedient talleys now wait and the numbers on my digital display were 12:39. I don't know what it was made me think of it but something in my metabolism pulled me into mathematics. 12:39. And staring at the arrangement I saw that the 12 as a total equals the sum of the other two: 3 plus 9. How perfect! Now when might this occur again? At 12:48, the two numbers would total 12 again and so on through the day every day there would be periodic displays of the last two numbers adding up to the first don't you see whenever I checked out the time, if the digits fell into place like this, the last two you get it, I could anticipate a synchronistic connection and lose all my what is this strange concoction I am drinking?" Her mouth becomes a curve of distaste.

We both: "I, ohh, it was.........did you see Host pouring.........is it all right or.........brandy something in..."

"Well, why look at me like that. I go through this regimen all day and it keeps me *compos mentis*. But I realized I wasn't just stuck with my bedroom timer oh no. Digital numerals are absolutely everywhere. You know. There's digital temperature readings, addresses on buildings, Dow-Jones listings, uh, FM radio frequencies, like microwave read-outs all there crowding in their little concert to predict my personal happiness. But in my bedroom, I have managed to live beyond the correct time as what I see on my clock is the relationship of all the chance variables on display. Therefore I can live in that room timelessly, I mean without caring about the actual hour." Her smile is splendid.

"So what's it mean when the numbers don't jibe for you? What do you get if everytime you look, there's no. . .I mean, aren't you just manufacturing synchronicity?"

"I'm coming back to that, sir! You see, I am so validated by the occasional but expected, complete balance of some of the times that it is perfectly pleasant for me to be in the present, the now, when it happens. Oh, somedays the utter ideal is there for me if I happen to spot just any harmonious chronological coincidence or like when I get up at night and the numbers are conveniently lit up. Many times, I mean. We are all doomed to synchronicity, gentlemen, chained to the pendulum of our mad clockwork, helpless to halt its swing. A kind of nuclear attack on the mind. Oh, and there's one prize that sometimes comes." She is absolutely embellished with joy.

We both: "And what's that?"

"Well. This is the best one. That's when the time is at twenty-one minutes past three by the digital clock. And it can be either AM or PM, you see. You're wondering but it's 2 and 1 make 3 yes, the last two add up to the first ok but, in addition, it's all descending numbers 3-2-1. Ohmy. Did I just say the words, 'in addition'? Isn't that synchronicity all over again you see what I mean you two."

Priest and I turn to each other with a look hoping the other one will come up with something.

"Such conformists you both are! Just think of my favorite painting. Dali's "Persistence of Memory" with the clocks that are melting over branches and over tables and bugs on a watch so that time is an artificial concept. I know Salvador Dali was imaging me when he painted those softening clock-pieces. Doesn't that tell you anything about my chronological interludes?"

"You have something there, miss," says priest. "Dali visited Freud, you know. And this would be right up your alley considering your therapeutic engagements, right?"

I offer: "And Freud agreed with Dali that the artist had succeeded quite well enough in painting the unconscious."

"So then memory, my memory?" She lingers in appraisal.

I decide to quote the queen in 'Alice.' "It's a poor sort of memory that only works backwards".

"Well, Hirsch, time is a measuring device not a realm in which you seem to abide." This is the cleric being less quixotic than I. "Spiritual life begins to decay when we fail to sense the grandeur of what is eternal in time."

"You're saying my obsessing over time is to be eternal?"

"Time is eternity in disguise, you could say. You are placing yourself in time rather than in space. Space is where you find holiness."

"You priests are afraid of everything you keep trying to explain."

"Women have a higher summons than we poor clerics. Inasmuch as behind the Almighty in the shadow of His cloak was the figure of Eve, already in the Creator's thoughts and the realization that man needed a companion." He elevates his empty container. Eve our first mother. Two sons and one kills the other. World's first holocaust" He smiles auspiciously, his eyes large, graceful, shiny. "Regardless, the Lord casts the cosmos and then experiments on a pebble." He regards his beer-mug. "'Cain's Wife' would be a great title for a book."

Hirsch's conversational elan is undone. "Cain......... had, uhh.........a marriage........."

He clears his throat. "The Life and Times of Eve," comes the preachment. "Almost the first thing she has to cope with is a snake who offers her only one fruitful chance.........You get that, Storey? 'Fruitful.' What wordplay!"

I'm laughing. "Right, padre! And Eve could only think, 'Where's God been? Where's He going every night?' She's saying, 'I have a naked man, a bunch of fruit trees, a talking serpent, no comfort facilities and You want me to go on a diet and give up apples'."

"Eve," continues the priest. "Her ageless temples. Always open for prayer and sexual feasting."

"You mean 'sexual fasting'," go I. "We all know that God remained a bachelor. But Eve. Evaline. Evaluation."

"Evolution," chimes in Hirsch. Something in her blood shadows her cheeks. "I wish I could deal with the available world, the one beyond the pendulum of all the mad synchrony—helpless to halt its swing—bitching up of everything, I mean." She is standing, intently eyeing the priest. "Is this a confession of faith, Father? I'm not even Catholic. There is this luxury the way you people practice self-reproach. Shrinks run the same game. It is the confession, not the priest nor the couch doctor that gives absolution. We only need to feel we have been forgiven to put the matter to rest, yes?

XXI

The door is banged open. Millie pokes in. "Get out here and make it snappy, you people. Since we're not going to be writers anymore, we're furiously trying to remember old poems and then we're to think up lyrics to give to Stone so while the rest of us go sleeping, he'll mix up some tunes for us. *N'est ce pas?*"

I follow her out as I hear the priest saying to Hirsch, "You know the confessions and the bread and the wine are only symbols. And, without faith, the cross is only wood, the baked bread, wheat, the wine, sour grapes...." while they both follow me to join the gathering.

I daresay the infectiousness of these six should stir up some soulful sonnets and such. But will Host's scripturgic-curing strictures affect everybody's one, final, literary, albeit metric creation? The purity of poetry! Like the last drink before rehab. Or the last kiss before shoving off. Or the last direful metaphor before getting on with the story!

It's Host perched on the oaken table. People have stopped drinking as they concentrate on lyrical matters while the turge-master urges them on. "So, you cleverdicks, we are ready to crack on to our destinies and with a not-so-hearty farewell to writers' enslavement, I would imagine. We shall just piss off out of it with something much older than prose, meaning poetry, of course. Come in, Father P and Miss Hirsch. Yes, take a seat, if you like. Shall I begin? All right." He clears his throat. "It may be a bit of a novelty but if we are going to spend a few mental coppers on lyrical poetry for Mr. Stone's awaited melodies, then shall we take up pen and pencil and actually—dare I say it— write the words down on paper?" He squeezes his features as if expecting a group riposte of dissent. Instead, all present regard everyone else with a sense of oneness albeit a tacit kind."

"All agreed then?" Host asks. "A fillip of composition. One final flourishment."

"A cocktail for the habituals. Perfect." puts in Freeman.

"Back to wasting our lives on pulp then," says Millie.

I get into it. "Host is only suggesting there be a closure by way of some creative poesy. It doesn't mean you have to gluttonize from the forbidden ink, as it were."

"Forbidden ink?" cries Millie. "Mr. Storey-man, are you trying to be a writer?"

"Nobody's perfect," is my rejoinder. "I've stopped writing, too. You don't have to be addicted to something in order to abandon it. Not unlike marriage."

"I never got to marry in any of my films." Doll knows the M-word, all right. "And which I always got the part of the sarcastic prostitute and I would end up in bed with the pizza-boy." She does her camera smile. "A director told me one time, 'Never marry anyone who won't give you back your clothes'." She stares at the curious *klatsch* about her. "What!?"

Freeman is rarely off-stage. "Here's a drinking poem I once wrote:

'Try a drink everyday
and all your pain will go away
along with everyone else
<he pauses>

So let's have a few more belts.'

"Jesus wept," mutters Stone, still at the piano. "I need more drugs if that's his groove. My brain is going somewhere under the keyboard. Gotta get on-beat with the resta y'all. Like lyrics only make sense if you want them to." He slumps down again, instantly looking utterly blank as if he were plugged into the wall with the switch off.

I go over to him. "Stay with us, man. There's still you and the night and the music."

"Irving Berlin," he says without moving. Then: "Only the sun will send me to sleep. You dig?"

"What makes you do it? Well, HOW do you do it?"

"All jazz is a search for another reality. Same as life."

"Sad, little, lonely, perfect brush of loneliness," chirps Hirsch.

Father Confessor rises to the moment. "I'm quite in the mood to offer my contribution to the musical scene. Call the tune, as they say. I should slip outside to the blessings of the night to commune among the twin spirits, that which is in the glass and those away in the galaxies. Oh, the stars and the catholicon cure all cocktail diseases. I know I'll see a light out there. It is the brilliance waiting in the despair. The Almighty shall be my amanu——uh, my muse. My endowment." His energy is somehow restored, "Jesus forgive me, I'll take a chance and not write about God this time."

Host manages a sprightly slide off the edge of the table. "Hey, you swots! Before we start splitting up, we all must toss out a little trial-doggerel just to get into the arms of Calliope, bless my soul. She was the Greek god of poetry."

"Mime and prophecy, too," adds the parson.

XXII

Host fairly gleams with expectation. "Creating lyrics for Mr. Stone won't be so easy. It will take time after we adjourn for the evening. But just for now, shall we try to amuse ourselves first by recitiing any nonsense poetry we've fancied somewhere in time. A few scraps of rhyme that come to mind that we can deliver if we try. Not the famous masters of poesy, I mean, but some snatch of whatever trumpery that will divert. Just for the moment. Anyway, I had a bit of fun memorizing this one."

He politely clarifies his throat several times into his fist. Then:

"The Englishman, if left alone
forms an orderly queue of one.
He thinks the amusement has begun
when he dresses in tweeds just for fun."

"Dear Host," says the priest. "That is so tomfoolish that I fear you have proved that God is indeed against art. Although let us realize that the Almighty has never consecrated creativity beyond the sex act."

Millie is radiant with rhymed souvenirs. "I always loved this one. Let's see."

"Bare earth..............mostly when crawling
sky ....ever so enthralling
depths......................only when falling
love me......................or are you just stalling?"

"That's so lovely," says Doll.

"Charming," from the *compere*.

I applaud with the rest of them. Whathehell. This is good sport.

Millie turns on me, "You! You would have a million jingles, Master Story-man. What's with your name anyway? Are you full of stories, after all? And what kind of stories, one wonders. Are you waiting for a wreath of leaves for your brow before you begin something Edgar Allen Poetic. One more and then it's your turn. I happen to know a verse on Pollock," she says. "Ready?"

"Jackson Pollock:
such an alcoholic
dripped his paint for frolic
never got high draulic

Just for fun, he dropped his paints
Then, so drunk, he dropped his pants
Titles, numbers, all by chance
Painted pictures, isn'ts or aints."

I'm completely trounced with everyone's rampant ingenuity but indeed I must come up with something. "There's a little one I actually wrote myself. It's, um…"

"Italian chef Caesar Cardini
mixed such a distasteful martini

We needed this ballad
to praise Caesar salad

Thank God that it's not Caesar's weinie."

This one goes over fairly well. Freeman loves it. Gives me a one-arm-around hug.

"Hear, ye, everybody, then. I got a martini one to match." It's Doll.

"A martini, like a belief
shouldn't be shaken

And oh! the relief!
when the smokes are Jamaican"

As he hears this one, Stone raises his shoulders and gives a loud, phlegmy cough.

"I can say," goes the priest, "that hearing frivolous poetry won't kill you. It only makes you stronger."

"C'mon then, parson. Whaddaya got for us?" is Doll.

He straightaway blurts out:

"The only way I can get philosophy to rise is to say Descartes stops thinking for a minute and immediately dies."

"Heavy, man," says Stone.

"Well," is all even Host can say. Then he spouts:

My kind of monk
an Asian philosopher
while driving drunk
said, "Sorry Ossifer!"

"Now that is, that is hilarious," comes from Millie as she glances at the priest..

"If you don't mind a bit of gaiety, here's another funny one I always liked," says Father. "Well. it's:"

"Now that we don our gay apparel
whose turn is it to be in the barrel?"

He ends this delivery with a detonation of his own laughter that only the corpulent can produce.

Freeman shoots a look of mock deficiency at me. "And we thought we were homophiles."

"Here's to poofters everywhere," says Host, raised glass of whatever is left.

"**More camp!**" cries Millie and seats herself on the floor, beckoning the other two women to follow her positioning.

The priest is on!

"You call that a gown? If it had one more feather,
you could fly
I see you've already decided whether
you should try."

"**Ta-dahh**" He manages to bow his entire magnitude.

Freeman is: "I got a really good nellie one."

"**Oh, goodie, do it,**" says the priest.

"**Really? Here it izzzz!**"

"Oh, please, Mr. Jesus
no longer tease us.
‹his voice is whispery›

Let our hail Mary's
release all us fairies."

The crowd roars. Who shall be next?

"**I am going to be absolutely fearless,**" goes Doll. **First she moves her lips in silent practice. Then once more. Then. "Okay! I got it! Now this is about love. So here it is. I read it on the wall of a ladies' room in New Orleans:"**

"Love is like a lizarrd
winds round your heart
penetrates your gizzard
then turns into art."

She giggles uncontrollably as if she's just heard the lines from someone else.

Everyone claps gaily.

Host is heard over the applause, "Well, we are surely getting ready for some serious musical lines for you, don't you think, Mr. Stone?"

The jazz-man has remained quite fastened on to the piano all this time. He looks up with a face gone white in a kind of formaldehyde gloom. "Cool then. It's my groove, man. All you people's poems are going to be my jive-lab of various boogie-bop experiments all at one time. So this is fer-shur saying that, that, after all, poetry is......... is........."

"Somewhere between syntax and rhetoric," I suggest.

Stone turns himself about on the piano bench and, facing the rest of us, begins:

"Jazz is sex
filling up your groin
heading toward that moment
when it's your turn."

XXIII

The place is now a chamber of stillness.

"I am reminded of the old canard about prose begetting poetry," interposes Host, quickly. "Because, as I said before, poems, not having logic or narrative, are much, much older than prose. And, without the burden of engaging in the logical or the narrative, poetics so coolly render for us the beautiful or the sublime."

"Yes, and…." It's priest. "….and little children devise poetic expressions quite naturally so there seems to be no culture, however primitive we think it to be, without a traditional poetry. Even the woebegone, juki-we Eskimos produce poetry."

"Absolutely! We should all feel deeply and gratefully sensible about the art of language," Host goes on.

"Not after today, though, right?" says Doll.

"The frozen ears of boredom," mutters Stone.

"Let's give the man some pulse here," shouts Millie. "I do love performance art. It's so pretentious. Isn't that what we're doing in this place? Hurling our dithyrambs. The promises of utter approval right on the spot without the need for galleries, agents, brokers, tax accountants and the rest of capitalism. Don't worry. This is still everybody's America, and I have been obligated to make as much money as I can. What a delight to love money! That is, until you find illness. Consequently, for a nightcap, Hosty-Toasty, I want your most aged wine breathing itself into the rich atmosphere of *cri d'espirit*. In which we are all at home. You know, sometimes......" drifts off on these words as she observes the designated *sommelier*, Sir Host, taking leave.

"The muse composer sits in the loneliness of invisibility," comes on Stone. He seems suddenly cool as jazz, alive to his wild, soon-to-be collusion with the lyricists, his *meshugany* bargain with the night. "I'll come up with a few scherzos by morning. You cats have the tough part. I get to do the music."

I say, "I thought it was the other way around. Words easier."

"Right, dude. Because music is the art of noise. Art with continuing plans. Music is time away from money, you know." He eyes Millie. Then tries a semblance of relevancy on his usual bland expression. "I'm one of those guys that checks out all the credits at the end of the movies while the audience is leaving the theater because there is major music still charming the air the sad composers have to keep on truckin' to back up the scrolling. Another thing about you writers you will always wonder how musicians do it." He touches out a few, complex chords, both hands selecting keys very close together.

"Wow!" says Freeman.

"You play?" I ask him.

"I thought I did."

MIllie bestows a high-bred smile. "Well, dear Stonerville, if you can play that well in your present fettle, your piano must be astonished,"

"It's jivey to be near money," he chances. "Bop doesn't pay well."

Millie twinkles her eyes. "I've always spent my money like a spoiled empress. That's the delight of it." She bows in self-amusement. "I love piano-players, though. They are required to keep their game quiet most of the time while others blow their ideas out to the world, right?" Stone looks more surprised than synergized as she goes on. "All I know about jazz is the cafes, artists, elegant lesbians, that certain atmosphere of intellectual ferment, as Fitzgerald said, 'where people go to be rich together'."

"I've had some time on the stage myself," comes in priest.

"Well, says Freeman, "There are only three reasons to become an actor. To shock your father, to impress your friends and to sleep with an actress."

"The stars are glistening with love," coos Millie. "Know where those words come from? It an aria line, translated, of course."

I'm: "Somebody once said opera is fine there's just too much singing."

Host speaks up, "People sing because they think they CAN sing."

XXIV

Nature or what's left of it calls me away. Whatever will I miss as I check out the facilities. I am not walking that well. Where am I again? Fictional life for me has completely become this cameraderie, the fugitive gang I have sought after, the delicious torment of being *alius dictus*. And I'm also very much on my way to the BR. Let's see. They are all kind of helling around, having a good time. Drink has become an important coinage of the evening. Everything now clear as gin. Writers seem to be such good drinkers. What's that old gag line? An alcoholic is a man you don't like who drinks as much as you do. Now here I am in the bathroom and there's that ridiculous face again in the mirror. Consumption of booze allows you to decide you are smarter, faster, tougher and better-looking than other people. God! the time I have spent outwitting those who might unpleasantly detect my substantial tipsy state at some given moment. Bartenders more than wives or police, really. But drinkers cannot help it. All of us have that point in time where there's no sense in going on with anything if you're not having another drink. I am absolutely in that present, incredible state. Now do I dare sample Stone's pharmaceuticals? Last time I did a joint, the next morning there was a hole in my clothing. I'd rather burn my hand than my trousers. My reflection indicates with its ridiculous concept of my eyebrow shapes that it is time to return to the congregants in the main room and hide myself in vocabulary.

As I open the door back into the set-to, the sound of bull is heard and not the papal kind as our Father seems to be into some spiritual realizations or ethical compulsions or cosmic inquiries possibly a little tangled for this hour of the night.

His voice is going on with ". . .an incompatibility between man's egotism and the Divine purity, The heart of good fiction is always religious. The faiths make up the codes and then the grim readers go leafing through the cognitive widgets and sprockets of storytelling. Of course, they never know in advance what they want from literature. They approach a work the same way they approach the possibility of falling in love, all their lobes and metabolism aquiver. And they are all in need of a story that convinces that history is the will of a just God Who knows them. We are living in kind of a post-Christian era, you see. We have seen through Christianity and now all we want is happiness."

Strange citations from an ecclesiastic.

"You have a good point," I say. "Years have gone by and not a single, new god has come to us. Are we bored with the same old Almighty and hasn't our imagination failed us or have we just become worshippers of the god of literature."

"Is there one?" asks Doll.

"Hermes is the Greek god of high, arcane literature." Host would know this. "If you want a god-dess, there's an Egyptian who was the patroness of writers and builders."

Hirsch has raised a forefinger and is shaking it. "Hera," she intones. "She was the goddess of marriage - commanding yet approachable - you invoke her to find that illusive husband. The entire milky way is said to have originated from her indiscrete splash of breast milk. Hera. And I am Hirsch, a namesake."

"And I am going off somewhere to write some lyrics," says Father. "Potentially for the last time." He shoots a valiant look at the work-room door for a moment. Then he bulks his way out.

Millie glances at the departing abbe. "Wearing black," she says. "Black every minute of their lives. Go be a priest in a blushing world. Actually I look good in black. Makes you look thin. If you're already thin. Would anyone mind if I tried the last bit of bubbly?" She moves to the oaken table and pours out the remainder of the magnum. Stone is the only one not paying attention to her. She regards him as if he is while she drains the glass. "Few composers are good pianists. Does this mean your harmonies won't be a joy forever?"

The musician does not look away from his keyboard. You'd think he had simply given-in to the demands of pop culture or something. Then:

"I sit down on the piano-bench and I open the lid." The once-stoned voice is at this moment clear and calm as a weather report on a sunny day. "The piano discloses its mouthful of scales, and the maestro transmits his forte, an itch in the fingers called improvisation. The other day, I came across a poem I had written as a teen-ager and I have recently put it to music. This won't rhyme or gratify. It goes:

"From my sailing craft
the sea's color is jade of east

(His singing is a thin tenor like a young boy's the melody discordant reaches for something the lyrics seem to own the very air ideas ticking from his fingertips seeking pursuing)

"pulled from an idol's eye
countless tongues, the lick of delight
beguile every wave to interweave

"the suggestion of a moon
begs its earth lovers to belieeeeeve."

XXV

I am about to start some applause but maybe just let the effects of his fleeting performance stay in the tiny silence.

Which his usual self freely breaks into. "I do my memories and all the jewelry of jump tunes. Didn't Ginsberg say, 'The dead have given us a chance to beat them'? Well, we're all together now. Am I one of us?"

"Well and good," says Host, putting on a fey expression, "And I must repair to the kitchen."

"And I to the powder-room," says Millie. "The artist must arrange her motives."

As she withdraws, I wonder if all the mental massaging going on isn't making my six Gabriels paranoid one moment and cured the next. It was their gestalt company I was in search of where I had no inkling of the common cause they shared in seeking a permanent writer's block. Dear Luigi P: I am an author found my six characters. Like yours, the players are turned into plotters of their private stories and emotions. Placing in their own hands the consideration of free will. Mygod! It's all about finding one's own worth! All of this, as homogenized, is the chaos theory producing in fiction the same as it does in science, a loose and traveling geometry. I'm a storyteller exchanging my roles. Composers become writers, daubers turn out great titles, vocalists write their own songs, architects become sculptors, decorators turn out to be TV stars, engineers are suddenly designers, artists mature into intellectuals, creators are reincarnated as being at one with their characters in all their role-shuffling fractals. But I am dealing with a creative achievement rather than with abstract constructions. I know I am mistaking novelty for merit. I also have had a ton to drink.

Hirsch has by now quietly seated her malignancies on the piano-bench with Stone.

Freeman meanders over to the piano. "Yeah, Stone, I saw your biography on the Cartoon Channel the other day. Hey, do some more chords, man." Stone lays down a few complex variations.

I can see that the comedian is dying to sit in, especially before Stone starts thundering around on the piano like some musical Jupiter. "Play something yourself, Rich," I tell him. "Stoner surely wants a drink or a hit by now."

The jazz-man looks up at me. He blinks absently and then gets up and goes over to the great table, Hirsch moving with him. Freeman sits down gung-ho at the keyboard and strikes the first few notes of "St. Louis Blues." My mind goes, "I hate to see……" He reminds me of Clint Eastwood's shtick in the few movies where the actor plays his own piano. The Freeman sound finds its energy in some soft boogie-woogie, the optimistic sense of the blues.

Doll sits nearby doing her nails. "Whenever I hear that song, I think of New Orleans."

"Goodbye, St. Louis, then," is my guess.

"I knooooo," she purrs. "Last time I was in Nawlinz, which is a real, alcoholic Disneyland…… like that?……anyways, a waiter wanted me to eat something called ravigote."

"Well, the classical cuisines of the Cajun palate—"

"You dippy! I'm talking about the waiter, not the food. I spent some time under a tray myself. To be a waiter is to pretend to be a waiter. They learn to become that way by doing their impression of uh, you know, of a waiter. They walk a certain style, strike a kind of attitude like not too intimate but don't be distant either. I prefer them now that they are calling themselves 'servers'. Many of them squat down to take your order and and sometimes they actually sit in the booth with you, especially the waitress ones."

I am standing in captivity so what the hell. "I view all servers as solitary, impatient, nasty-minded, brutish, preoccupied and careless."

"Professionals are bores, I agree," she says. "They have no other topic. They're all such easy game. When I was tending bar one time, a guy who always leaves coins on the bar as a tip suddenly brought out pictures of his kids. One look and I told him, 'You have such beautiful children. Thank God your wife cheats.' Man, those photos went back in like a shot."

We both do a vulgar snort. Lord, I have created a Sheba.

"Hey," she goes, standing up. "Two old men are close to their last days and decide to have a last night bash on the town. So, After a few drinks, they end up at the local cat-house. The Madam takes one look at the two old geezers and whispers to her manager, 'Go up to the first two bedrooms and put an inflated doll in each bed. These two are so old and drunk, I'm not wasting two of my girls on them they won't know the difference.' The manager does as told and the two old men go upstairs to do their business. And then later as they are walking home and take a break on a park bench, the first man starts a conversation as follows:

'You know what?'

'What?'

'I think my girl was dead.'

'Dead? Why do you say that?'

'Well, she never moved or made a single sound all the while I was banging her.'

'Could be worse. I think mine was a witch.'

'A witch? Why the heck would you say that?'

'Well, I was startin' in with the sex act and kissing her on the neck and I gave her a little bite. Then she farted and flew out the window. Took my teeth with her'!"

I'm hysterical. She curtsies demurely. "Speaking of waiters, I'm going to check out our own chief server in the kitchen."

Wow.

XXVI

With Freeman absorbed at the keyboard, it's now me and the last two, Hirsch and Stone, Unplugged. He is dragging on the final possibilities of a joint, she holding an empty glass. He is on fire by now and she the absolutely absorbed listener. "During a jazz gig, most of the time is spent listening to others. To know the essence of a thing requires us to go back to its origination because time erodes every moment. I mean, man, what is swing really? It's how to treat audiences. Everyone knew the church music and red-light songs, and inventing jazz was a way of singing the melodies through a horn that made all the instruments sound human."

He's a little slouchy, talking. She stands erect, saying, "It sounds so lonely. I hear you but each player is alone with his concepts, right, and it's all that waiting your turn and then it's, I mean after all, it is called a solo, right?"

"That's cool, babe. For a chick, that's cool." He loves her jibe. "But okay. Artistry, man! Artistry is developed in privacy. There is a need for aloneness which I don't think most people realize. When I'm on, something momentous shudders through me and the jazz rises in its be-bop dream. The darkness and the promises. You guys want a J ?"

I go, "Pot now will put me to sleep." Hirsch keeps her *maudit* face in composure. I go on. "Let me ask you, man. There's the percussive part of piano-ing that Dizzy liked. The fingers strike the keys which is something beyond the sense of the ideas and the creativity but also what the instrument can be commanded to do dynamically beyond the notes."

"Groovy, doc. I have sat at terribly ruined pianos in the kind of exo-bars and intro-drunken, killed, stretched out nights but oh so many lost forever perfect chords which is the inimitabully...the immitabill...for chrissake the hot shit of being alive for so many moments and the assurances of all that jive-eternity. And to get on the track, Jack, to find at least one single jamtime where the beauty goes on beyond the end because there is no end just everybody being gone beyond There."

Freeman finishes up his keyboard improv with a stock Ellington riff. Stone applauds him. "Groovy, dad!' he shouts across the room.

"Yeah," goes Freeman. "I don't play anything up to the Stone. I'm gone before he starts. Ohmigod, last time I sat in somewhere, the moon, comin on the national anthem and what will I do when it's my turn going when it's How High The Moon and I know the chords but not the intricacies of being intricate Each person gives himself to those he finds in life." He picks up his empty glass from the floor and smacks a kiss at me. I go over to pour him something as he starts to play again. It's "In A Mist," the extraordinary piano number by the trumpeter Bix Beiderbecke.

"He plays the piano, yes," says Hirsch, "but it's the only time he uses his hands for something other than holding a glass" as she gets back on point. "I made the mistake one time asking him what he was getting me for Christmas and he said to me, 'You wouldn't drink it'."

He keeps playing without looking up and says, "Alcoholism is the only disease you get yelled at for having."

"Fuck you dot com," pronounces Hirsch.

Just entering, Doll now begins to clear things off the table. "Women are saying the fuck-word same as the men do," she coolly states. She gathers up some debris and heads towards the kitchen. "Will somebody please press REJECT?" She backs out.

Hirsch glances at Freeman still playing and then smiles crookedly at Stone. "How do you people do jazz?" she wonders. "'Why don't they ever want to stop?' is a better question." She claps her hands in such delight with her little *bon mot*.

Stone closes his eyes, apparently fixing some thoughts for her. "Jazzmen know to take in the melody for awhile and then it's your turn to find a way through the lust-busts of jive your instrument does its sentences but the brain can't stay long on something everyone else knows about the melody it's moments of loss and verbs of trial then lungs of performance and you can feel your intimacy with something everybody thought was lost and that second chorus you take because you are going going and your place on the bandstand rises with abstract brainstorms now it's the knowledge about being right that shoots through like insulin of the soul such expansion way past God now He's diggin too and that nobody ever died in the middle of a jam session nobody ever lost his beauty on the way to the end because there may not BE an end the drummer knows this as all the rest are leading him to the possibility of a few riffs drummer's a purring cat in a rusting cage of skin and sticks and cymbals the earthquake of beat like you said, Diz played piano just to do something his mind needed to get percussional thoughts into his trumpet squeals time becomes notes, not just beats, you dig?"

"I wonder if music helps writers of fiction," says Hirsch.

"There's the songs in your brain when you aren't playing but everything is incessantly there because somehow it's got to be and if composers, say, can steal music then you can cop on something your brain needed to get yourself into yourself. Also about jazz, it's that keep going thing, keep doing, keep hitting on something that is perfect from your horn or your ax or you being present and don't give in when the session ends."

"Jeesus Christ!" shouts Freeman.

"You know, Stone," Hirsch says, "I am maybe into your little candy of love thing."

"Ice cream," says Freeman.

"Hey, keep killing your liver." she growls, then goes on, "My life, Mr. Stone, is so much more a point-counterpoint kind of fugue like all that gallery of lost music you men take on. You're always saying everything is gone, don't you? Like gone, maaaaan." She has mimicked a male voice. "Like composing in the moment that you put yourselves in touch with your unconscious as well as conscious state. You getting this?"

He moves his head side to side as if to shake up some spirituality. Freeman is now going for the kitchen. He gives me the finger and a huge smile as he slips out the door.

Hirsch sees him. I tell her, "Well, I can see you're going to have to scratch me off the list in your gay husband's wallet."

She ignores my little pseudo-nellie thing and talks on. "I want to chance my mind staying as the thing that lets anything happen past the stupid loss of self and the gain of another day but yet a kind of opening in the brain that lets happiness out. That's when the mental typing tells the reporter of life that all is well again if there is even any need to examine it."

Stone's physicality takes him over as he stands and raises both thumbs-up, waving his fists. "I am digging you entirely," he says, as he strides about.

I myself am not completely getting her. I had this person as a character who was only mentioned without ever appearing on paper in the *mise-en-scene*.

"Whaddya think, Mister Narrator?" Hirsch eyes me. I say nothing. She puts on an in-charge look. "I am the most assassinated woman in the world. I've been ignored, endured, removed, rehabbed, found asleep somewhere, convinced by a dance instructor that I would be a professional ballerina and then, having roomed with a couple of Latin gals, found myself determined to be a Spanish translator and so went off to NYU when I met Freeman in a he-she bar somewhere in Manhattan, actually exhausted him with sex and got him into quite the cyclonic marriage because of that and then down I come with my manillia and cystitis infections."

"And therapy?"

"Oh. The shrink said I was raping the couch. Said, I mean, she told me I simply lacked the power to modify my own consciousness. Psychiatrists offer interpretations. They don't realize it that patients want relief, not opinions. And that damn Freud wants everybody to convert hysterical misery into common unhappiness!"

XXVII

whoa. Small w. So much her! "I think you have an obsession based on love," is the best I can do. Maybe I could change the subject. Slightly. "Well, you know, meantime, our pal Stone here keeps emerging from his metaphysical depths while you, Miss Hirsch, are constantly backsliding into your own." They both involuntarily cock their heads at this. I've got to keep on. "Yes. You've subliminally met in the middle, one briefly coming up to be free and the other going further down to co-dependency. I would call this syndrome a psychological treadmill you're both on. And the only peace for either of you comes from being at the piano for one of you or from the affair with synchronism for the other. But what's so terrible? It's music and it's clocks keep you two away from that undercurrent of dread everybody's so ashamed of sensing."

"But the trouble is," Hirsch argues, "that when I'm far from my neurosis and I take in the taste of the air and the murmuring trees that say oh we will stay the same and yet they grow new lies. Nature will not let us understand it and how depressing that nothing natural ever dies the trees stop the winds and they keep on growing themselves from the top down into the welcoming vagina of the ground. And see, nature doesn't care because God is working on his daily sense of nothingness. There!!"

All I do during her verbals is to think of my guy Biely's line: 'The trees talk up their secret reverie and a new rush of time flies into the past.' Whew. I should try some Gaudi on her. "You know, the trees can be our teachers," I begin. "My favorite architect Antonio Gaudi once suggested this notion about growing things. And also when he would design structures, he refused to join walls at right angles. This is you two, joined at all odd angles. Gaudi once designed a dressing table that featured an intentionally lopsided mirror that made any symmetry impossible, while the base of the glass suggests the movement of a running animal. Also sounds like you guys."

"That is a groove," semi-apprehension from Stone.

"One cannot help it when the house is going out the windows," is pure-Hirsch. "So say some more!"

"Well, Stone fails to sell insanity and you Hirsch succeed at it. He times the beats at his keyboard, you beat time by living in a digital display. If I'm to go on with this, I may need a drag after all. No, just kidding. But you have both freed yourselves from bondage to the empirical world, opening up the glorious capacities for abstraction. Freud calls this internalizing process an advance in intellectuality and credits it directly to religion."

"That cat was all into sex, man. You know, a far-out time was when I was sixteen I tried out a call-house and I was totally confused and, like, unacquainted and I was going to have salvation with *beaucoup* chicks. The, uh, the mysterious possibilities of lies and sex, of cocktails, boobs, hairdos, dancers. And women. The most important rhythm section for cash money that there is!"

He looks at me, possibly expecting some OK male sign.

Hirsch says, "We gotta sit. This is much better than my head-shrinking."

We find chairs. I'm first: "You know, it was Freud the medical-man who declared himself utterly incapable of experiencing pleasure from music. He said some rationalistic or perhaps analytic turn of mind made him rebel against being moved by such a thing as harmonies because he couldn't stand not knowing why he was affected."

Stone says, "He should have taken up jazz piano so he could hope the vocalist would become his lover." He mugs at Hirsch.

Hirsch goes; "You won't have to bother your hormones over me. The only song I know the words to is "Mack the Knife."

My turn: "I don't want to know the words to it. I just want to understand German theater." I heard that line somewhere. Oh, well.

"Poor composers are society's fault," says Stone.

"Yeah, well, stay on key," I give him. "You have to write music all night. As soon as everybody comes up with some lyrics."

"I got serious chops, Jack. As far as nighttime goes, my sleep comes to me in a red hood of poppies. Or when it rains, I can hear the spattering on rooftops of all those many, many, falling notes. And screw anybody that don't dig my tunes."

"I see you'd rather be a warning than a good example. Maybe Hirsch should sit atop your piano. She could look as if she's going to jump."

"Make it happen," she says, maybe not really getting the humor. "I have heterophobia in the first place, a suspicion of all others, you know." She sounds solemn now. "I think like a child back when I played in the sandbox. I kept looking to see if I had developed a true understanding of sand." Her serious expression with absolutely nothing to discover in her face is all that helps me restrain my total panicky gut-warning of do-not-permit-thinking-of-any-possibility-of-uncontrollable-laughing-about-to-go-into-hysterics that I suddenly feel. I can only hope something please god anything the least amusing will now be said by either one of them so that I can really burst out in total guffaw from an entirely different provocation.

I try to hold my breath and then, not a moment too soon, Stone offers, "I watched a TV documentary on drugs." beat::::::::beat "And it's the best way to watch a documentary."

I explode with imbecilic yukking into which Stone joins me in obvious delight at the supposition that he has just been extremely witty. Oh, what saves us poor, incorrect, unpurposed, saturated kibitzers from being called out to explain and justify ourselves? The sextet experience gets better and better.

XXVIII

Hirsch stabs right through our hee-hawing: "I'm confused, though. No, wait. Maybe not. I went to New York University. I know things. Einstein was mass in motion varies in space and time. How's that? Also: the amygdala is a small region deep in the brain that processes emotional content, especially fear and anxiety. But, ha, you do not need the amygdala to realize that you cannot actually really see space. Or time."

"It feels good to open your mind," is the only sensitivity I can extend to her. "We all cling to things and to situations and also to people because we've dwindled into them. We know exactly how certain people will make us feel, especially when the response is guaranteed to be ugly. And anybody new affects you exactly the same, right? So why not just be satisfied with probing into someone absolutely worthwhile?"

She gestures unenlightenment by raising both palms. "Into someone absolutely worthwhile,"

I repeat. "Yourself." She still looks insensible. "You're a woman who has nothing and still wants less. Something aesthetic can't help you because you don't have that amazing energy for art. You've had no success in attempting to join the world where everyone is occupied so it's just you being mad in outer space all alone. You're a child with one toy and it's broken. And, you know, if you wrote the story of your life, its title would be 'Who am I?'"

"Maybe you're right," she does her cunning smile.

I continue, "The only way for you—- No. Wait. The honest way for you is to let go of your attachment to outcomes. Just practice letting things be. Only actresses get applause. But think: obsessions have a fashion quality, you know; fancy them as one of the things from a fabulous wardrobe you love to dress in. Caprice can sparkle. There are a thousand ways to be dreary."

"Yes. Dreary and empty. I'm afraid to laugh or cry. That depraved man has taken away all my maps. I don't know my origin or my destination like a radio with the volume stuck at maximum and all the stations vanished. Why is love so goddam dangerous for me?"

"There is no love, dearie. Only tests of love."

"She's flunked," comes Stone.

Hirsch being my only minor creation, I have no handle on her, and thus, prose with her will have its constantly new requirements.

"Why don't you just leave Freeman?" I say.

"I have, I Have! I HAVE. Every goodbye doesn't mean I'm gone, though. I did begin to notice his faults which I would never have forgiven in anyone else. Do you know this man on the wedding night stood on the bed and he was wearing nothing but a jock strap and a sailor hat? He thinks that humor is a dead-on aphrodesiac!" She gets up suddenly. "Do you want to hear these things?"

Stone and I just sit. She looks around and then: "I haven't told you about the welcoming company of Three North. There I was. In the abyss of an entire, crushing mental-hospital where everything is permitted and nothing is heard, Because all you do is listen to yourself rot, and, you know what, in the wards, the mad people sleep just like the healthy ones do. And those who were seen dancing were thought to be insane by those who could not hear the music. It would drive a psychopath back to being normal. I can tell you it was a place to forget your name and what you are. I learned to wait for whatever would break through my depression. Once reality is gone, you're certain that your entire life is also screwed. But!" She inhales a great draft of oxygen, holds it still for a moment. "The doctors soon stopped paying any attention to me at all and one day Freeman showed up to get me released and when the news came, I dressed quickly and there I was for him, posed in dove-gray chiffon."

She reaches down and touches my arm. "Don't worry. I'm just the damaged mouse the cat toys with. Maybe we all need our enemies. Actually, punishment is over for me. The crime though remains mysterious." Pause: "I've got to find a bed or I'll start sleep-depriving myself into some semblance of mania."

She opens the door to the kitchen just as Freeman is coming out. He scrunches around her as she exits, smirking at him on her way. "Still in there giving all the vampires heartburn, are we?" she says sourly. The door closes.

The funnyman looks at me. "What did she have to say to you?" he attempts.

"I donno. We never got very far," I reply.

"Trouble is she is so convinced she's some character people will want to know. I felt so bad when we broke up I went out and bought her a trailer." He plumps down at the keyboard. "All right. The world's full of dangerous and smiling chances. Like me murdering the piano again." Sighs. He regards me with his loaded mischief. "So there are two things for you, Mister Mysterious. Which one will be first? A preposterous joke, here's a sample: Receptionist says: 'There's an invisible man in the waiting room, doctor. and the doctor says: 'Tell him I can't see him!' Orrrrrrrrrrr. Instead of a joke, you may have from me the story of 'My life inside a condommmm.' Which will it be? And no cheating!"

"I'm going for the joke."

"Just cuttin' out, folks," announces Stone. "I gotta have fresh air for one of my lungs." Heads outward,

"And now………that long………dark coda………
into the night," he mumbles, exiting.

"Talented, cracked-out hippie, " says Freeman. We
both smile.

I say, "The joke you're dying to tell? C'mon! If you
can't be yourself, who will?"

"I try to be a writer but nobody's perfect, or did
someone already say that? Okay. Guy dies and
goes to heaven and there's a long long line of
people waiting to get in. Suddenly, as he looks
way up the line, he can suddenly see everybody
dancing and jumping up at the front and then a
great big cheer and all the people up there are
celebrating. And those in the back are waiting and
asking, "What's all the shouting about? What's all
the shouting about?" as they holler up the line and
finally the man in front of him gets the news and
turns around and says, "Good news: Today they're
not going to count fucking."

Freeman has game here. I'm chortling. "Super
joke, man," I'm helpless at his humor onslaught.
I love the raillery. "And, uh, what the hell was the
condom thing you had for me?"

"Yesssssss. It was my life, you fool, you!" He
squints as if contemplating the miscellany of it all."
Are we alone here? Are the microphones and all
the recording machines off now? I went to college.
I was in bop city. And a passing fiancee became
a marriage. Then suddeny I had a trial offspring.
Then the ho-wah. Would I be a good father! Okay?

Right! Have I been a nurturer or have I spent my time existing on stage instead of developing my parenthood. I come from a family of entrepreneurs who gave me an education on how to express myself, sell myself to customers. Advertising. The family business was waiting for me in extremely sound circumstances. I became successful as I dealt with clients, not personnages. I learned more about their intricacies and financial sheets than many of the sponsors knew about themselves. I had to learn to ally with them but also in the process I defined myself. A schmoozer. The golden way to come into comic existence. Adrift on a bare stage with the world paying to get in so they can have one single, solitary emotion. Laughter. Yeh, the sensation that competes with that other climax everybody wants. With laughter, both genders get to have multiple orgasms together and no apology for it. No shame, no mess, and, best of all, no obligations." He reaches for a drink and sets forth on some rhapsodic personals.

XXIX

This man Rich Freeman knows himself. Why didn't HIrsch get on with such an enjoyable character? Or better, why *couldn't* she? At worst, he would have continued to be the only anchor she had and at best, she would experience a share in his whimsical utopia. Instead of infinitely proclaiming her loneliness as a right of ownership, she'd have been in a somewhere. He did philander her into a place that his activities eventually became a notional dream-world to her. But sometimes, a woman will just sift through the ruins of infidelity, as with Hirsch, and then stay, and keep on staying around and psych out the worst possible jailhouse for herself: love. The losing argument and the winning disclaimer. She imagines she is seen as a heroic, a woman swirling in some monstrous, melancholy, isolated whirlpool. Hirsch can't even get wise to her misdirected desires by way of Buddhism. Freeman sees jokes in everything. Hirsch can't accept that she is one of them. He has no guilt over an undeveloped marriage. She has no guilt having connived so long at disregarding her psychoses.

I'm half listening to the comedian's bio through his accounts of business and comedy, details my creativity left off the accounts. Somehow you can catch what a person is saying but still let your thoughts speculate.

"......and I matriculated but did not linger at many colleges. After all, what does produce a comic, his conflicts or his panache? Certainly not academia," he's just saying.

I should get into it. If you don't throw in any questions, it's usually a long time listening. "So, uh, what was the first——"

"What got me started? Yes. Once when I was a passenger on a cruise-ship, the professional comedian in the ballroom did his nightly turn and afterwards, I spotted him on a stroll around the deck, and so I stopped him and we shmoozed a little and I decided to tell him a joke I made up just to maybe amuse him. The joke was a guy has to take a test to get his driver's license or something like that and there were three questions that you had to answer. Number one was 'How many days of the week begin with the letter T?'. And the next was 'How many seconds are there in a year?'. And third was 'How many D's are there in Dixie?' Then I gave him the answers. And it is that there are two days of the week that begin with a T: Today and Tomorrow. And there are 12 seconds in a year: January second, February second, March second, April……And there are 137 D's in Dixie. DEE dee dee dee dee dee dee dee dee DEE dee…" Freeman is Dee dee-ing the melody of the song. And says, "And when I finished the first onslaught of the dee-dees, this experienced pro had a baffled look on his puss and then he says to me, "Are there really 137'? This comatose response from a paid comic on a luxury cruise! Jeez! He misses the entire joke! I tell you, Storey-dude, I really needed a spa moment after that. So, dig this! I find a party deck with bikini-babes in the pool right there for a nice round trip. And I actually picked up on a chick at the diving board, left her for a few minutes and went off to get some cocktails and when I came back with the drinks, lesbians had taken over the entire swimming hole."

We're both laughing as I go, "Where is the love?"

"So when it happened that the crappo, professional comedian was so depressingly un-hip, I bought a jug at the bar and went to my stateroom and immediately began writing all the humor I could think of whatever I had heard or what I could make up and kept on boozing till it occurred to me I didn't have to invent the wheel either and went off to the ship's library, found some joke-books and a star was born!"

"I hate to ask but where was Madam Inquisitor all this time?"

"She spent our entire holy matrimony never figuring anything out while I was learning to order the right martini. And it is not easy, my friend, as you may know, that, on first taste, this drink is indistinguishable from anti-freeze. Oysters on the half shell. also required. Plus the real goddam caviar without the salt, baby. Then it was the arts! Oscar Wilde and Leonard Bernstein, for crissakes. After them, there isn't much else. Oh, and Marcel Duchamp, the guy that put the moustache on the Mona Lisa. He said she smiles because she is aroused. Anyway, all this was so I could become someone else. Preferably Melvin Douglas or William Powell or, at least, Franchot Tone. You know, the guy in black tie, always talking on a white telephone, which the *maitre d'* has brought to the table."

"Well, the way you speak is the voice of a writer, I must say. Being cured of scripturgia may not be......um." He cocks his head that somehow stops my comment. "You are such a writer. And so just tell me what lyrics have you in mind for Stone to make some music with?"

"Ahhhh." He puts on a handsome smile. "Not just the words, my dear contestant. Our grand prize will be awarded in advance, next on the Rich Freeman show!" His tone of voice has changed to deep and full, sepulchral, 40's, network-radio announcer. I think of Arthur Godfrey's guy, Tony Marvin. "Realize," he continues normally, "that I have composed the music as well. This means you and I, at least, will not have to wait to learn if

Stone is a virtuoso or merely a quixotic. You like that?" He sits at the piano and hums indistinctly. As I try getting psyched up for the man's musical composition, Pirandello's theatrical words roam my reasoning. What were they? Yes. "Creatures of my spirit, these six have already been living a life which was their own and not mine anymore, a life which it was not in my power any further to deny them." I don't remember if it is also his quote about nature using the instrument of human fantasy in order to pursue her high creative purpose. Anyway, my own intimate narration is now poised beautifully. I have found the capacity to transcend an everyday world and generate some colloquies, some psychodynamics, a smattering of autobiography and actually some performance art in my fugitive world. Even now, the comic at the keyboard will be giving me cause to deal with another aspect of creative achievement. Rather than with trifling, abstract constructions. Okay. Freeman will play and sing his own dittie now. He will be purged of jokes and taunts and ribaldry. He seems ready to speak before he sings.

A long, dramatic throat-tuning. And: "Before I begin my song, you need to know that I was arrested once for staring fixedly at young schoolboys." He looks up, haughtily. "They were stealing my hubcaps while threatening my chauffeur with a giant bookbag."

"You, sir, are as logical as a burning fire-truck! And bad manners, too."

"Wilde said such was the infallible sign of talent." His voice changes. "Good evening! Permit me to introduce myself." He is now the Carpathian Count. "I am Dracula from Transylvania! I just had my tongue dry-cleaned this morning. And I can't do a thing with it!" He thrusts out his tongue several times in a sense of being ineffectual. "Remember, my friend: a pint a day……keeps Elsa Lanchester away. You are seeing me now in living death."

He plays a continuing, pounding chord with both hands to set up the beat and then he is singing to his own accompaniment:

"When I was a freak in Transylvania…..
I was hired for haunting houses,
And at night when someone drowses,
I would start with my carouses
Like a vampire should."

"First I'd get my chains and miscellanea….."

<Mygod, he's rhymed 'Transylvania' with 'miscellanea'! Brilliant!>

"And like a dream from Walter Mitty
I'd appear with my black kitty
Plus the rest of my committee,
And the news aint good."

"The victim in the bed would start to rise,
And she would notice the mascara on my eyes,
Plus the pomade in my hair
And the fancy vest I wear
Made her slowly, very slowly realize:"

"I'm much too beautiful to ever be a vampire.
With this cape and tie a vision
And my spats on exhibition
I'm like Mandrake the magician
But my act won't swing."

"If at night you should decide to turn your lamp higher.
And there's something not quite human
That has risen from the tomb an'
With those fangs it aint Paul Newman
But it don't mean a thing."

"I never scowl, I never even scoff.
'Cause if I do a piece of makeup might fall off.
But as Lugosi often said:
'It's better bled than dead.'
And, lord help me, if I ever start to cough."

"Frankenstein was just a crazy doctor.
And the monster that he bore
Could never get beyond the door
Because those square clothes that he wore
Would never fit."

"Doctor Jekyll was a wild concocter.
He drank some old Kentucky pride
And changed himself to Mister Hyde,
And then his practice up and died
And that was it."

"Lon Chaney played the wolfman with a zest.
And when the moon came up, he stripped down
to his chest.

All that hair is so damn gaudy,
Has to shave his entire body.
With those slimy fangs, he ought to use some Crest."

"In the opera house there was a phantom
Who was told by William Morris
With that horrid face before us
You could play the role of Boris
Goudonov, if you please."

"On the list of monsters in this anthem
Is a mummy who has been in
Fifty yards of rotten linen,
And he hasn't had a gin in
Centuries."

"M is for the million parts they gave me.
 O is for my open coffin lid.
 N is for the needles of injection.
 S is for the suffering of my id.
 T is for the tomb of Jack the Ripper.
 E is for the elegy I sing.
 R is for the resurrection nightly on TV"

"Of Boris Karloff, Vincent Price, Eric Von Stroheim,
Peter Lorre, Emil Jannings, Sidney Greenstreet,
Charlie Laughton, Georgie Bush,

and that well-dressed monster,
Little Old Meeeeeeeeeee!!!!!!!!!!!!!!!!!"

I can only show astonished applause at his clever, waggish performance. "Hoo-rah and bravo!" is

what first comes out through my clapping. He offers a ghoulish grin. I say, "You shall have the best wine in the cellar."

He bows as if mockly refusing the crown. "Can't you see?" he responds. "I want a man who can transform me from a refined socialite into a cockney flower-girl."

"Maybe we need to march right out of here on some mission with burning torches, the ones in the Frankenstein movie, the, uh, the avenging mobs with the cudgels that fired up those perpetual flames."

"We should go find my old residence," he announces. "One reason I left Miz HIrsch was my former son 35 years old and still living at home holed up inside the room he was born in. The unforgettable words, "It's a boy" are still festooned over the top of all the windows. He stayed in bed till noon. Whenever I checked him out in his room, he'd have the covers pulled up to his bearded chin. And, and always one unconcealed hand holding a comic book in front of his face. Also there would be the blood-curdling music grinding enough to dissolve the paint from the walls. I had to go in there and look under a ton of candy-wrappers and cigarette papers and female-bondage mags and find his earphones and establish them onto his huge head and he would always smile sweetly and mouth 'thank-you' as if I had just placed a dollar-bill on his brow. At night, of course, when everybody else was in bed, he would bring home the most obnoxious people. One time, to get rid of them or, at least, endure them, I went down and I unlocked my liquor cabinet and opened up some Crown Royal and they got so drunk, they became my dearest friends and I got a chance to insult them about their boring lives and kept them laughing for hours. Where am I going with this? The hell with me and history. I've lived through conflicts and a DNA of the damned………"

He is suddenly talking under his breath in what seems to be a spurt of single sounds. "Puhh, puhh, puhhh.

"Why are you muttering," I ask him. "I mean, is it something that just happens to you, like bleeding gums?"

"Only trying to get all the bad words out," he sighs.

"You lack that Samarai resolution," I offer.

"Ah, to learn what your children will become. That is to say, the identities of their ultimate defeats. Of course, there was his mother in a cartoon academy and his father attached to a microphone! Ohyeh."

I keep him going. "Microphones only belong to sufferers anyway, don't they?"

"I'm not going to lie about it. My life's an open book as it is. No comedian can possibly keep anything secret about himself. I mean, our most private and our most dangerous intimacies become heroic statements any chance we get. Miss Whozis was perfect for me. Neurotics are tough to live with but they provide great ideas for inanity. Just stick an 's' in that word or, uh, take out an 's' and, uh…."

"Yeah, I get it. So go on about Hirsch. I spoke to her earlier. Her chief interest as a co-dependent is in making you feel………what?………"

"Guilty?" he offers.

"How can you possibly metabolize the strange cocktail that she is?"

"This person lives in the anxious tense or didn't she say that?"

"She said she wrote in the anxious tense."

"Listen, pal. Illness is her life. And her unwavering reliance upon it has raised mental illness to the rank of a metaphysical state. She is unaware of anything unless she's actually doing it. Thus, ladies and gentlemen, is unleashed her willingness to be unlikely."

"What's the shrink say about all this? I mean, do you go with her or did you?"

"How many couch-jockeys do you want to talk about? How many incompetent, impotent note-takers do you have to see before wanting to cut your throat? Hey! Here's one you'll like: A psychiatrists says to his patient, "You're right there is a man following you all the time he's trying to collect my bill.""

I'm laughing wildly. Drunkenly?

"Thanks," he goes. "I am obviously the slave of an internal power stronger than my self-esteem." He gives a kind of needy look. "All I really want is to make everybody laugh."

"Getting back to Host and his scripturgiacs, then your only occasion for writing is to lay away some jokes, right? Forget Authors Addicted."

"I spend so much computer time tapping out one-liners I forget where the meeting is. How are the typing fingers anyway so easily in thrall to the process of stringing symbols together?"

"I know. I took typing at sixteen and to this day, I still wonder what's the point of having the letters so scattered as if a madman had taken over the English language."

"Typing saved my life, son," he tells me. "After two high schools and three colleges, I took one, minor elective way back in prep-school that did me the most good for the rest of my life. A six-week course in touch-typing! What else for a half-assed boogie-woogie player? Anyway, it was the Korean War and me in the National Guard which got federalized when things heated up and we were destined to go fight the Commies somewhere in Asia but at the camp in Indiana where I was taking basic training there was a hospital for the returning wounded and me the typist and a good speller got a gig doing medical dictation while everybody else went overseas to fight our nation's enemies."

"You in the National Guard? Wait! Don't tell me. You had one life to give to your country but you wanted to abuse it first."

"Somehow, as soon as we got to camp, they filled up our outfit by drafting a ton of recruits, 90% of them complete hillbillies. It was the wrong place for a smart-mouth in the middle of all those hayseeds who thought they were supposed to bring their own guns!" He smiles and rapidly nods his head up and down. "So yeah, I was in massive culture breakdown but my parents, man, were in a state of shock that I was actually in the army. The fact that I really didn't mind that much made them hate it all the more. I forgot to tell you it was my dad who, unbidden, signed me up for the Guard because he heard it was conscription-proof. And then they federalized us, for crissakes. Anyway, I got a job at the camp hospital as a medical stenographer. That's all I did for two years while everyone else went off to get shot at. All my educatioin but it was that course in typing saved my life. I even felt unthreatened enough to get married."

"Couldn't stand success, huh?" I urge him further.

"Yeah. Guy's got to get laid and those Indianapolis whores would only screw in the dark. I was getting more black ass than Sonny Liston. I had to stop sleeping with harlots. And besides, the rapists were ruining money."

"What did Jimmy Roosevelt once say? 'Those rotten hookers all keep givin' me the clap'." Freeman cocks his head at this, trying to remember. "All right all right so anyway, the marriage," I plead.

He's ready. "We newlyweds rented a room off-base in a farmhouse and it was great scoring every night until I discovered I had teamed up with a clinically dejected woman who took to her irresistable bed because that was the premier place to enjoy her illness. Sanctuary underneath the covers. The Gothic kingdom of depression. And, you know, this kind of shit, there are never ever any_clear signals sent out for anybody to work on."

"I see she does Zen,"

"Zen fails her because it cannot teach you anything until you actually aren't anything. There's not always just nirvana, you know? Freedom from suffering. Transcendant knowing. Luminous consciousness? Then there's her insidious codependence customarily accessorized with clinical gloom. Do you hear me? Gloom! One hundred and one percent all the way to hell as the bitchy, little kill-joy succumbs her way down to feelings of frustration or something existential. And. On top of that, she has a complete willingness to be unlikeable."

"The gap between frenzy and what?"

"Reality. Maybe. She can't wake up to that simple, elegant illusion that she should just live another life. She truly believes she is the most stifled woman in the world. Where did she get started on this? I don't know. She hung around some Hispanic *chicas* at Brenau Academy for girls and then went off to New York University to major in medicine, become a doctor, which lasted five minutes and that's when we chance-hook up somewhere in the Village. The sex was good. Let's say, frequent, which got me into this monsoon of a marriage."

"Well, dearie." I take in lots of air. "You married her. While you were still jagging around in the Army. You might have realized you owed her something outside of you being so busy playing Sargeant Bilko to the mentally unaware. Didn't you think to pay some spousal dues. A little attention to her illness? Tell me you did love her."

His eyebrows go up soliciting me to some of his wounded innocence. "I admit to dreading a certain cold space in my bed nowadays. But *amour du jour* is completely undetectable when you're annoyed. And could I, I mean, how could I love someone playing games with time and infinity and everything ends up being lost?"

I tell him people's lives fall into oblivion when they are entirely handed over to others. And that the mad clockwork of both their lives proves there is no useful future for each moment gone. Maybe this is too deep. Of course, he's doing a joke on her. "The woman even cleaned the stove before she stuck her head in the oven."

"Was she ever suicidal, though?"

"Yes, actually, among my grim recollections—I call them 'the deads'—I remember when she kept buying pearls, quarts and quarts of 'em, and declared she was planning to announce the exact day she could be buried in these beads. That was just before she dropped out of space and time altogether. She was then seeing a lady shrink and after many sessions, I phoned this therapist for an appointment myself to see what she could tell me about my wife the patient. See? I did try."

"So what happened?"

"The old she-shrink was extremely hostile the minute I sat down in her office. Whatever deariedarling told her about me had obviously so intensely charged up the psych-woman's emotions that I was regarded as just another abusive husband become absolutely villainous, and that I needed to be major scolded about it. And. While I sat there getting zero enlightenment, she took two phone calls on my dime. And, yes, bitch did charge me for the hour so I had my rights, goddammit. When I did ask her about suicide, she of course had no eyes for specifics re her patient and launched into the impractical claptrap of the trade. You know?" He puts on a dramatic face and is conjuring up for my amusement what becomes any, old, British, film actress playing Lady Bracknell. It's: "You see, my dear, doing oneself in is all just a chawnce to seek love and devotion in death that was soooo elusive in life. They say suicide is merely a fawntasy of dying without death. It is very interesting that......" He pauses to check out my receptivity. "...... interesting that in our thoughts of self-destruction we are not required to enduah the guilt over what we have wreaked." He coughs into an imaginary handkerchief.

I so enjoy his fakery and respond with: "Yes, a therapist can be tuned so exquisitely into the nuances of a patient's feeling as to be virtually paralyzed to intervene."

He's: "I can forever hear Miss Melancholy saying, 'Let's not waste time here. I have come to reclaim my husband.' Me. I was just no good at the kind of therapy she needed every, single, god-dam day. Especially if I would have to lie down on the couch with her."

I keep on him. "I'm just going to say that this little ingathering you folks are having here will change its dynamics once the other two females decide to provide you with some heavy shit about how you're treating your ex-wife. All women hear the same-sounding invocation with some kind of common ear. They are dangerous people when defending the wrongs one of them might have done. Always remember the male creed: being right doesn't mean you win. I'm just giving you a little hint for your subconscious.

"You say you spoke to her. What did you talk about?"

Time for a drag queen line (three fingers to forehead warding off imaginary migraine): "She pointed a finger at me and demanded to know if I was hiding some big secret, and I told her I was extremely suspishusss of certain of her husband's feechurzz. What do gay men do on the second date?"

"WHAT SECOND DATE!?" we respond in weary unison.

"A lifetime of listening to disco music is a high price for us aging queens to pay, isn't it?" he declares.

I see his delight in fickleness. We men all have our inner *grande dame*, I guess. A gaudy, old, lewd something. At this moment, I find it difficult to recognize Freeman's purpose for signing on with Host's rococo routines in the first place. This comedian has been on a long, lifetime march just to take in a few straight-lines or perhaps discover a commiserative listener for his marital rants. Ah, the icy forests of self-deception.

He's on with another joke. "...so the teacher says, Clyde, your composition titled 'My Dog' is exactly the same as your brother's. Did you copy his? No, ma'am, goes the kid. It's the same dog."

Our laughter quiets down at the return of Stone from the outer darkness who begins talking without even looking at us the moment he closes the door. "I actually had a total vision out there, dudes. I mean. It was a trip."

"What'd you see?" we go.

"It was The Death Of Pot," he says, in a terrible monotone. "I know, I know, but dig::::I have had this haunting feeling that pot is dead, man, and its funeral is attended by myself as a tragedian::::burial goes down in my backyard where the winds of love carry off the remains of a lifelong affection::::there is, there's a brief eulogy in memory of a thousand mistakes and a million assaults on the brain matter::::pall-bearers storm theimagination::::regretsgounchallenged::::police cars blare their siren benedictions::::importers and dealers kneel in their betrayals::::for the first time, thunder is clashing before the lightning flashes driving me inside to the better vices::::and it is now at last, that I am cured of all my scripturgia and will write only music::::"

Freeman and I are applauding lustily, during which he gives me an aside: "If we could only convince him that getting crack is not all it's stoned up to be." Stone rather slinks to the piano bench and begins to play the ump-chuck chords to "Chopsticks" one-two-three, one-two-three and then shouts out over and over in rhythm, "Where are the lyrics oh where are the po-ems and where are the writers, those musical show'ems, oh," He keeps vamping along in three-quarter time and motions us to join in his whimsy and we do chime in with him as he leads our singing, having paused first with a big: "OOOOOOOOOOOOOHHHHHH......where   are   the lyrics oh where are the po-ums and where are the writers, those musical show'ems...." as we two idiots join in with his little, cockamamie show. Soon the comic and I are waltzing about together and soon the kitchen doors open and then the workroom opens and out come Doll and Host from the one and Priest and Millie from the other. all waving their vaunted, poetic creations and strutting a few individual, choreographed improvisations. As Doll pirouettes to the piano and ceremoniously places her handwritten lyric beside Stone at the bench, each of the others follows her initiation—Host, somehow the last, inventing a mad-marionette flounce, his hands waggling at his sides—and all drop down into various chairs. Priest gets the comfy one.

Stone finishes his piano-ing with the Loony-Tunes-That's-All-Folks musical ending. Then silence. Host gives Freeman a watery smile. "Well, Sir Sondheim, I am on fire in my respect for your creativity, meaning have you indeed in our absence, already handed your own personal lyrics over to Mr. Stone? I am sure he will want to provide his compositions for all in our little group, yourself included. Sometime tomorrow, shall we expect then, Mr. Stone? And now, your contribution, Freeman?"

"Ah, yes, But I intend to provide my own tune for you all *with* my own sonnet tomorrow. Words AND music by yours truly." he vows, giving me a wink. "It's only music. The basic noise of life,"

"Music is what keeps the credits alive while moviegoers are leaving the theater," I offer, picking up on something earlier.

"The only art that makes us sing," says the priest.

"To me, music is waiting and wanting."....Doll.

"And willing,"says Millie. "Just imagine life without song, and you'd have no patience for the other arts."

Host says, "Ah yes. And if anybody laughs, the symphony is ruined." He glances about. "Well. Shall we say goodnight and shut down the chattering cocktails and leave the maestro to his one true god? How ever will you come up with all those melodies by morning, Mister Music-man?"

Stone is staring at the piano with only his brain seeming to roam the keyboard even as he answers. "I know the angry fix and I am hip to the catastrophe of love and maybe put the two together. I think of music anyway as composed on the tongue, you know?"

This seems to be more than enough for Host. "Now for the rest of you lot, just follow the walkway past the gazebo to the guest-house. Plenty of light and towels and bedrooms, three on each floor, gentlemen up, ladies down. Oh, dear, have we lost Hirsch?"

"Check out the nearest bed?" suggests Freeman.

"Lord save us, in this humble residence, there's just my own four-poster. Except for, um…Let me go and investigate. He's quickly off through the kitchen in search of the missing miss. The scripturgiacs rise. They are altogether played out. Myself as well, I guess. My hours have gone from cautionary to bold and somehow past the dangers of disapproval and, by some means, to the far side of my fantasia. I am wondering if Host will have a trifle or two of energy for a very late chat. Here he is back with Hirsch in tow. She's all small from underneath one of her scarves. "I am seriously late," is all she can mutter. Better than one of her immediate frenzies. Obsession is supposed to be forever.

Host intones, "Let us disenthrall ourselves for the nonce."

And so. Now for everyone. The priest, bulky and sleepy-eyed, seems quite ready for the "miracle" of all the ordinary acts like breathing, belching, relieving and definitely sleeping. Total detachment from worldly pain and pleasure. He sets himself before Host and bows his ponderosity. "I would take my leave of you, my lord. That's 'Polonius'," he clarifies.

"There is nothing you can take from me," begins Host in perfect response, "with which I more willing would part. 'Hamlet'."

I say: "Except my life. 'Rosenblum and Gildenstern Are Dead'," is my contribution which came out of Stoppard's play even as no one present seems to know this, including my capricious variation.

But at this moment, there is no better drama than a drunken Priest possibly going to declare his status at the curtain of night: "I am the Jerusalem of Catholicism," he does announce as he holds the outside door open for Millie.

"And I," her cultured tones are sounded in instant rejoinder, "....am the Vatican City of atheism."

"An atheist is someone who doesn't believe in his own beliefs," announces Freeman as he follows them out, Host touching a wall-switch which I can see softly lights the edges of a pathway for the retiring guests.

Spying Freeman heading out the door, Hirsch rather pops to as if the fancy of dramatically pursuing him into the night could develop for her an invitation to new pretence. She lingers at the portal saying, "Ah, another tomorrow. You know, some mornings, it just doesn't seem worth it to gnaw through the leather straps." She clicks her tongue several times, holding both eyes tightly closed, deeply deliberating, and then departs. Night air pours through open doorway.

Doll stands up. Through it all, she still flows out her spring-fashion magazine-cover look. She daintily touches the pouty, little mouth but no yawn comes forth. "I don't know why I'm not feeling sleepy. I guess I'm too tired to find out.. All further knowledge this evening will definitely depress me anyway." She checks the room for a moment. Then, "You all should know that after a stint walking the runways, we models have this perky, little shrug at the end just before we turn away. Watch me." She pimps it, then saunters outside, without any notice of the unclosed door.

Host goes to the threshold, stares out for a few moments into the dead of night to see the bedward-bound troupe on their way. "Now spurs the lated travelers apace to gain the timely inn," he intones.

"The first thing I think about when I wake up is sleep," comes the voice of Stone, still in semi-forgotten, musical obscurity at the corner of the room.

Then it's Host over to him at the piano and solemnly shakes Stone's hand. "Goodnight, dear minstrel. Liberate all the free verse you can by morning. Storey and I will be doing a little, liquid rehab in the clear night air of abeyance. You will need privacy," he suggests, pronouncing the word with the British soft "i". He twinkles at me to detect any suggestion of abandonment. How can I really? We hear the inaugural sounds of Stone at once pounding out a few strident chord progressions, Host flips a wall-switch as we slip out to stroll toward the beckoning light of the gazebo.

XXX

"The supper of the heart is when the guests are gone," says he, taking my arm, seemingly to offer the assurance of a developing epilogue. "Those secret calls of the darkness," he whispers. "A special kind of silence." He carries the ubiquitous potation along with us and we are soon seated in subtle comfort, the night and the wind our sole ambience. He passes around the elixir and finds us a couple of cigars, fires up a lighter that flicks into a huge flame, and we both puff our way to the perfect glow. "Ah, the poets!" he declaims. "Let them be well used. One could say that they are the abstracts and also the brief chronicles of the times." Eyes now bright with confidence, he takes an extravagant draw on his cigar, "So where are we, leo J?" blurting out my given name as if to begin a chat on some intrigue we are both subtly well-aware of.

My cigar is an excellent smoke. I take a deep, knowing pull. Exquisite. "Don't tell me these are Cuban?"

"Yes, they are. Have to sneak 'em in, bloody boycotts. You Americans have made exiles of yourselves, first transplanted, as it were, from our domain and now doomed to sterility. You go into ecstacies over what you won't allow yourselves to enjoy. Good job we let you try out our scotch."

"The Scots make good whiskey and also good poets like Bobby Burns. But I've never been able to drink enough so that I could really quite understand him." I must match my host's erudition.

"And how's about our six versifiers. What do you think of them, so far?" he asks.

"These people are in bondage," I make plain. "And they envision becoming fugitives from writing. I would think that to cease dashing off novels or screeds or even lyricizing is not to lose all possible interest in life. At the same time, there's a sense of sadness in their literary retreat. I feel I'm in a fog of writers. But I can see by your lecturing that you—and they—are going to rearrange reality. Imagining......fantasizing......yearning."   The cigar smoke drifts like a dream through the soft lighting.

"Well, enough of obscurantism," he goes. "I've kept them trapped in the drawing-room all evening. They are surely beginning to feel like Israel. First victimized and then punished for it."

I cough on my cigar. "Uhhuh-ahum. Let's see what we can make of them. Your technique of weaning them on poetry is to be the last episode. I mean, they did dash off some lyrics before saying goodnight. Somehow the psychical Stone will be absolutely brilliant with show-tunes and ballads by sometime tomorrow. I notice that even you, kind sir, joined in with a contribution, and I know that Hirsch donated to the experiment. Undoubtedly offering her usual esoterica. One thing all writers are interested in is how the others do it. Same as the people who can sight-read music will always marvel at how other musicians can instantly play anything they hear. Y'know? A few notes of any tune, a scrap of melody and they find instant *metier*. And then the very same jazz-musicians that can chime in to a jam session with nothing but the talent of a ready ear to do their improvisations, they are mystified how anyone can look at some sheet music and perfectly, instantly rattle off the piece without needing a single glance at their hands on the keyboard."

He's leaning back on one of the huge pillows and softly blowing out the Cuban smoke as if the opacity will assist his abstractions. The brandy and Cubanas mellow us both into an air of aristocratic nonchalance. I urge him further with his memoirs, supposing to afford him the utter escapism of reciting some keepsake experiences. Any dreamer can happily charm an audience of one, especially when wit and style overthrow substance. I always crave amusement more than information. But, oh, that tireless breed of talker who blackmails the listeners into accepting his piteous, autobiographical excuses in detailing his endless failures. And all those tales of love with blame never accepted. Never even acknowledged. O brave old world that has such people in't. Coming this fall Version 2.0.

Now he speaks. "You know, there's a lot to be said for the *extempore*. You bring me to mind when I was a five-year-old, I was with a lad a bit younger than I who asked me to read the daily comics to him from the newspaper just arrived at his house. Myself I was not literate enough for the task but his keen wish to be entertained prompted me to observe the storylines of the day and concoct my own dialogue to fit the cartoonists' drawings. We spread the funny papers out on the floor, got down to our elbows and knees and so I began at the top. Oh, I was quite familiar with the British, comic-strip characters I mean their lives and their fortunes and peculiar antics. So it turned out my rosy-cheeked audience of one was quite content as I spun my bits of whimsy over the entire cast of the Sunday funnies, and I can say the formulation of stories and personalities took me through quite a mental saraband. Not unlike the creative musicalities you just described. Afterwards, I wondered what the effect might be upon the lad when his old gaffer came home and read him the actual comics."

It's going to be a shame for me to offer up even the slightest, meager sentence but if I remain silent, he might feel as if he's over-lecturing. What I have to relate seems nocturally bizarre enough. So. "Once long ago at a jam session," I begin, "they let me sit in for one, long ballad, and later after the evening's gig, I credulously went with a bunch of the musicians into a middle-of-the-night, Russian steam-bath. We joined say a dozen other naked men sprawled or seated on three tiers of the main sauna. There was a pungent fragrance of smoke from the wood embers used for heating up the place to what felt like boiling temperatures. I was new, never tried it but slowly coming to a gradual feeling of myself installed in an ambient, hellish domain. Then, at a sudden, sweating, feverish instance, everybody silently got up, took lots of towels, and we went elsewhere in the bath-house and each of us in turn was to lie down on a massage table and in came these massive Slavics with sprigs of birch I guess it was and flayed our backs to accelerate our bodies' experience. Invigorating? I'll give it that. Ever to be important to my life? Not!"

I should really tell him that I want somehow to discuss the six characters before too much consumes us or probably quite the opposite. Although in the light of our garden kiosk, I see his keen face eager to put more edge on our conversation.

"My dear soul-mate of the night," he goes. Ohboy. He will speak. "I have often traveled continental Europe and must offer my own tale of hot stones heating up a steam-room. Of course, it was in Finland and I was touring Scandinavia with a friend and we ended up in a serious sauna. One of a million bathing enclosures which that culture makes use of. So, the difference in my story from yours is the damnable practice of familial bathing which meant that when we were invited to partake of the sauna and had gone naked as directed outside their little hutch, we entered the bloomin' spa and directly into the presence of several members of extremely plump, Finnish families all in the nude, you see. Well, it was too late for formalities and worse for the slightest glances at the great-bellied corpulence in array and I am talking about the women, Well, smiles all round, they knew we were English and seemed delighted at our discomfiture, issuing a few, shared, chuckling remarks and welcoming words in our own tongue. Well. They bade us sit. We did, careful to cross our legs, which brought titters from the few ladies present including one really *zoftik* young miss. My sheepish, perhaps longing perusal of her abundance quickly dissolved as someone of them arose and, to my horror, was pouring cold water upon the heated stones, producing an infernal furtherance of the already steaming atmosphere. No! shouted my brain. Are they mad! A way to melt down intruders? Yet smiles of a summer sauna was the only indication of anything nefarious. How quaintly ignorant we travelers were. it happened to be September, mind you, and the baking and roasting was only step one."

Host knows he's got me by the tale and takes a grand toke from his *habano*. I tell him, "You know Freud smoked cigars until his life ended at 83, and! He was in a morphine-induced coma to relieve the pain from his cancer. But, forgive me for cheering up the conversation. Do go on. You were being broiled in HEL-sinki."

He laughs in delight at my jesting phonetics. And onward to speak: "So there we were, *en flagrante*, heated to absolute succulence in Sibelius splendor, All I had left in my nakedness and personal violation was a very weak comprehension regarding the possibilities of survival. Gradually, my body began to endure the horrors engendered in the mind. It appeared I was unharmed, engaged, as it were, in the attainments of another society. Well, we two sat back, even deigning to uncross our legs and began casual conversation with the younger,

English-speaking inhabitants. At one point then, my companion whispered to me something about not forgetting the next ritual, something about a plunge into a 60-degree bath but I assured him these folks were too jolly-good genial, et cetera, for such daffing on two kindredly agreeable guests. Well, I can tell you, in short order, all the Finns smilingly arose together and made as to depart the premises and we two likewise, grabbing up our towels in shared relief and, courteously as possible, waited for our companions to pass through the door. And as the portly, young woman passed by us she said that we could just leave our towels behind."

As Host pauses for a sip, I amuse myself working on the *double entendre* of the word 'behind.'

"Well," he continues. "As I mentioned, it was just turning autumn for these locals but was indeed the dead of winter for us poachers. Thus we emerged, expecting to walk back to the house and retrieve our clothing but instead....what sight we had previously ignored now greeted our burnt-out eyes! Finland is not just brooding forests and lakes but heaping bloody mountains of SNOW, massive piles and blankets of broad-lying, frozen precipitation. And then, I tell you, when each member of the family in total *deshabile* was one-after-the-other having an actual roll in the freezing bloody mass...! What?! My partner quick-glanced at me with a look partly of fear but mostly out of betrayal, my previous self-assurances now dwindled.

"Ouch!" is all I can say to him. I can almost feel his chill-sense coming into the clear night. "So go on," I encourage.

"There was nothing for it but to accept this glacial baptism, throw myself in and get the bloody exploit over with. And that I was the first to go was considerably more a show of martyrdom than of bravery.

"And?"

"It turned out that the thought of being immersed in snow was rather worse than the actual contact plus the sight of the exuberant others helped with the prayerful plunge. So it was a very slight and undeserved sense of accomplishment the finishing up the entire ritual at the bottom of a sloping hill that brought my self-esteem up quite a bit, especially when I saw the Finlandians scurrying back to the now extremely inviting swelters of the steam-hut. All inside now were laughing most heartily at the expected finale endured by the new initiates. Ah, heat, safety, life newly cleansed down to the very soul."

We both sigh and I opine: "The sad, plaintive, lovely years of foreign travel. The explorer lets fall whatever caution he has been cultivating and goes pathetically into a wilderness of warning. It takes the Finns to teach us to forget the fear of being naked. But here I always thought that the British tend to consider the heroic a person who doesn't have any ambition." He offers a weak laugh. I go on. "Which reminds me of someone telling me that lunch in the Eiffel Tower was a must because it was the only place in town where you couldn't see it." Both chuckling. " But I will say that the best part of Paris-ing is the smugness of pulling it off. Events for me all shaped up one last afternoon near the Seine that the house of Picasso would get the once over. It beckoned the intellect once again to the chore of solving the mysteries of Pablo. Or not, which is the point, I guess. How far away from modern art are you supposed to stand?"

"Right-o!" he trills. "Now I'm in Florida, I couldn't give a toss about anything continental. We British say Europe ends at the Channel. Our side of it, that is. I was whizzo at living in the English countryside. After all, we natives have had to survive the terribleness of the weather not to mention our past imperial horrors plus the misfortune of the cooking, lack of clothes sense, dislike of great colors, ignorance of foreign languages and our instinctive conservatism, provincialism and imperialism."

"Please don't leave out your loyalty to your fellows and your courage in wartime and your Churchills and your Turners and your Plantagenets and Shakespeares and Lady Di's, too! And another attribute of you Anglos was bartering. Can one ever quite describe those vaunted Hollanders way back when their Dutch East India Company was doing its business of war, torture, immense wealth and, um, nutmeg! Yes, my dear sir, nutmeg! They wanted this spice so much, in fact, that they acquired the nutmeg-laden island of Pulo Run, one of the Banda Island chain it was, from the British in exchange for the entire colony of New Amsterdam which your predecessors renamed New York. But to trade away an entire, new world for flavorings! Besides, everyone knows that nutmeg tastes like a mix between cayenne pepper and grandma's basement. "

"Right you are, old chap. You Americans are always very generous about us fallen aristocrats. Still. Do know that I've settled in the right place. I'm a Floridian now," he moans. "Can't you hear my southern accent? If I want to replicate the dullness of England, then it's the flatness of Florida which is so boring that it is not favorable to art or poetry or even opera plus the monotony of its Atlantic shoreline. All you can say for this state is at least no melancholy winters. That this place is beautiful hides all its failures and what a great reason to want to live here!"

"Ah, yes, mein host, but consider that the greater world of Florida lies beyond its coast where the grand Caribbean Sea scrubs and washes its islands. And what a place to have a boat! As passenger, I once sailed the Grenadines and found myself on board with two local crew. They had intrigued me with their story of something called the green flash. It goes that on the tropical high seas there is a natural phenomenon at the time when, at the last second of its late-afternoon presence, the sun drops from sight just at the horizon. Of course, the three-hundred-sixty-degree world affords the sailor's complete view of the flaming orb that suddenly, after its daylong journey, leaves the sightline quickly once its oval-ness is about to disappear. This eclipse, oddly enough, doesn't change the brightness of the day but the last instant is said to be accompanied by an odd, green flash and perhaps a distant pop. One is not always on board at that time of day but my eventide moment to see for myself finally came and I in my most skeptical but anticipatory mood intently watched the golden globe as it rather quickly descended for the day and as the

last little arc of it sank into the horizon, I looked
and watched and almost prayed but was unable to
see anything green or anything at all. Had I been
duped? The old landlubber tricked by a couple
of sea-dogs? But, no, I was assured that one day
soon we would try again."

Host appears to be keenly following me, his forehead
by the spare glow seems discerning and strange,
precognitive. "So," say I, "that day came not long
after and I perched once again on the very prow
of the boat at afternoon's end as the tropical sun
performed its ritual. And then. As the last sign of the
yellow rim slipped down into the sea, here it was:
a green flash! Just a millisecond's worth but there
was no doubt as the verdancy left its momentary
proof on the pale-blue sky! I saw it! The green
flash! Was it pure imagination because I swear it
seemed to me that the scintilla of viridescence was
accompanied by a short pop of a faraway sound,
something to verify its clash from sight."

"Good story!" exclaims my companion . "Do go
on! Tell some more!"

"Then there is what the islanders call 'see-through
rum'. This involves a mixture of two, local, fiendish
ingredients. The rum is the product of the sugar
cane that is squeezed right from the pulp, aged
molasses, you see, and it is 43% hootch. And that's
the alcohol part of the libation. Then, one has to
find a fresh cocoanut. There are barefoot natives
willing to scale a palm tree for you and knock down
a perfect specimen. Next step. A hole is popped
through the hard shell husk and they then take a
good portion of the clear rummy extract which gets

poured into the cocoanut to merge with the milk inside. Now, this liquid is just a kind of water, that is, the condition of the stuff before it can qualify as, or I should say, mature into milk."

"And so how was it?"

"Not too bad. You can't distingish the rum ingredient. The nutty taste is so overwhelming and then also you don't think you're getting drunk as you continually raise the container-nut to your lips. I carried a damned cocoanut around with me all night from native bar to beach parties to hotel verandas and found the best way to secure it was to keep my thumb in the hole when I wasn't imbibing. Also, you can't set the damn thing down on a table as it wants to roll over on its side and spill its contents if left alone. Anyway, the joke is that next day around noon-time when I staggered my way from bed to brunch, I ordered lavishly from the menu and discovered as I swallowed down the fresh orange juice that the only taste I got was that of a strange, woody, leathery something-or-other which completely permeated my taste buds, overwhelming any ordinary, citrus expectations. I was willing to blame this on the service or the hour or my brain and so immediately dove into a great, perfect pile of pancakes, thin and lightly browned and doused in maple syrup and whipped butter. And, behold! No matter how many bites I took, the flapjacks had the exact same flavor I experienced in the orange juice, that of, yes, now I recognized it: cocoanut. All Cocoanut! Everything cocoanut? Expecting to cleanse this entire disposition from my altered sense, I drank the hot tea as if to scald away these effects and as my mouth recovered from the scorching, there it was, conquered still by the fiendish, oval nut flavor. And, yes, the evil libation would even infect a simple glass of ice water. Not to mention my morning-after thumb now white and wrinkled ugly from the long-night soaking. The only cure for the entire going-native with the locals was a wonderful man at a nearby tiki bar who knew just the curative in some native, cocktail mix. And here I am again, dear Host, marinating the night away in good company."

"Let us then drink the blood of our enemies," he growls as he pours the last of the cocktail into my empty goblet and leans back within a cloud of cigar-ness. The brandy is strong. The smokes are intoxicating Time now for my squadron of six? Have I indeed renounced my at-large, former existence in order to know theirs. Host's insights can be engaging even more to the point than my own. He's well into their ransacked company. I am the fugitive placed at his *porte*.

"Well, it was really swell of you to invite me along," I purr. "Was it just today? And so, let's us…I mean, here's a verbal nightcap for you. I'm just going on my intuition but, after all, intuition is all about seeing into the present, isn't it? These characters of yours—or should I say 'ours'—it's as if all through this entire day they exist in a tale by Dostoevsky. No preliminaries. Just everybody's intimate thoughts as stuck in moral nobility. Only our six are all just stalled in their own psychic traffic jam."

Host surprises me by continuing to look absolutely wide-awake attentive. "Do continue," he heartens me. "You haven't become too epic. So far."

"That's what's so swank about this scripty world of yours. This entire *forte*. First of all, each one of your guests is rare, singular, a stranger on earth. You know, Stone was telling me if only money were shared the way dope is."

"When did he tell you that?"

"I really don't......uh, my puny mind......"

"Ah, the effects of amnesia, What were they?" as he takes a quip sik. I mean a quick sip. Oh brother, how am I managing? He supposes something affective from me and I must deliver it without letting slip my credentials. I begin, "To Stone, the rest of us live in a world of stoplights and picket fences while there he is within the progressive music medium. He sits in the marvelous wrongness of everything, that vulnerable huddle of sounds. And unless you are into the music, you are unable to speak that language of theirs, the words of jazz alienation and improvisation."

"I wish I could plow a little jazz myself." He means "dig". He pulls out a couple of fresh cigars.

My soul is humming its existence now, whatever that means, and I've got bios on tap yet.

"*Chin chin*," he goes, firing up his stogie.

The only consideration in my mind is to down a further dose of blankness and venture another of the six characters on him. I try: "If I were to see Doll as a fictional creation, you know, she would be perfect playing Shakespeare, you see. She's right there for Henry Four. Falstaff vows to find a wife in the stews, they call it, the local brothels, and he has a relationship with none other than someone named Doll Tearsheet. How perfect. Doesn't even have to change her name."

"Righto! And think of 'A Doll's House.' Ibsen. The sheltered, frivolous and empty, um…."

"Well, the Ibsen doll-woman's name was 'Nora'. You know. But, uh, anyway, this is that our Doll breaks it all down with saying what she thinks before she thinks it. To men, she is one of those pulsing and urgent miracles."

"Yes! Charming!!" says my benefactor. "Girls that play the Heddas, the Noras, the Cleopatras, et cetera." He pauses. Closes his eyes. "But what of love? You never mentioned———"

"I say she can't know when a man is in love with her because she's busy being so ice-queen superior and slut-whore all at once. Doll comes a cropper on romantic love and so she also misses out on the tragic parts, which are the most interesting ones. Still you have to wonder about yourself when she's around. You get that swoon of sin in your gut. You know, what the hell, life is a chance to ruin love or did somebody say that today."

"She does seem to have her eye on everybody's reproductive system," he offers. "Not that she doesn't have her own fertile crescent."

"Yeah, she's got the curves just waiting around for men who've got the angles. Hey, we're good. We should be writing these down! Oops! Birds like her who have been photographed to death develop that look-at-me attitude. And she's still at it. . .most dancers, strippers, nudies have to retire around age 40. Then they go on endlessly trying-out, desperate to stay the way they are. You can navigate their waters, chart and consolidate their territory, maybe a worshipful measuring of the gradient of the breasts, the generous contours of other places, the longitude of skin. But their presence is just God confusing us with happiness. I once fell immediately in love with a beautiful, local actress appearing on a Pittsburgh stage and that very moment fancied myself entering the drama she played in. This captivating thespian couldn't have had any idea that she would be the inspiration for a screen-play I had always wanted to try out.

XXXI

"A screen-play? Really? What's it about?"

I actually got as far as FADE IN: EXT. STREET—DAY "After writing those five words, I was immediately seized with an incredible urge to check my email or clean up my work area or play something on the piano. I one time saw a picture of a chimp at a typewriter accompanied by the words: "Is anyone in America not writing a screenplay?" Anyway, what's our take on Millie the millionairess?"

"Millie seems to know that money can be rich in mischief. We'll see how it plays with abstention."

A muffled sound, possibly a small animal stirring in the night air, distracts Host for the moment. His head is turned, stiffly alert. I'm thinking I really shouldn't get too dark on him here. The world is full of loss. That's what keeps it going. Loss and longing. Nothing left to try. "What is Millie then?" I put to him. "A child of privilege who will be supportive of the disenfranchised?"

Without looking down, he taps out a huge cigar ash. He counts on his fingers. "Heiress, muse, political idealist, refuses to be defined by her glamour or, for that matter, by wealth. The thing about rich is they have all those options. And don't you enjoy the sound of her laughter? She's exudes that same utter charm you experience when a female opera star laughs in real life. I can only assume Miss Millie's sexual energies have not been lost to culture."

"She's a Jewess, you know," I tell him. "Not a particularly obserservant one, it seems. Ah, the high posh nature of it all."

"Quite. I wonder what our dear padre and she would care to discuss if left alone together. He'd have a lot to say about the Jews, I should think."

"I'd say the Christians did not become Jews because they did not become christian."

"Good! We must get those two in a *tete-a-tete* tomorrow," he says. "Can't wait till they start talking about the pope."

Now we are getting somewhere. "Our padre is such a high-voltage messiah. His retreat from literariness goes quickly to religion which *is* an art, isn't it? Religion is the art that has the most prestige because everybody can claim he's into it, don't you think? And aren't you leading them all to the healing power of art? They are to be aroused to the dangers of writing, are they not?"

He looks pleased at this paean to his relationship with them. "Yes I am, indeed. *Malgre lui.* 'In spite of myself'. But back to our clergyman. For our priest, art, like religion, idealizes nature, which one could say rather pleases God."

"Right! And God doesn't take sides. He just seems to keep the natural world in balance. It must be a struggle for a priest, I mean the fact that man wants neither God nor Christ. He just wants the authority of the Church. All that wrestling with existence and meaning and death. Poor God. Creation was such a production nightmare."

This line makes him smile. "And," he goes, "I have a joke for Father. Do you think I should tell him?"

"What could it be?"

"Nietzsche stops thinking for a moment and dies."

He exhales a draft of Cuban residue while the witticism sinks in. Then, the deluge of laughter pours out of both of us as the gist of God-as-dead philosopher sinks in.

"Perhaps our priest's conscience is getting confused with his faith," he chortles.

"The clouds and phantoms of religion."

"He's out to affirm himself to himself

"The only critique of paradise is paradox. And be there drinking!"

"Speaking of which," says my companion, "In order to keep this conversation going, do we need to sober up?"

"You don't mean hot coffee, do you?"

"Actually, no. In the cooler here, I have some lovely ice water which I find sobers the plumbing of the mind.. Just water, yes. One's system continues on with its swallowing and thinks the alcohol is still flowing but there's only water to calm everything down." He fills two tumblers with ice and water. In it goes. My mouth is dry, and the cool refreshment is perfect for that task. Even as my deepest soul craves continuing narcotic.

His hortatory is still strong. "Now let us take up the possibilities of the talented Mister Stone. What a piece of work is he, the combination of drugs and creativity. We discussed didn't we that the comglomeration of being buzzed helps the artist because madness is supposed to be a prerequisite of the creative process. Just think. From the hurly-burly of his mental world to the flagellatory aspect of his music. What did he say? Jazz is gems?"

"He called jazz the jewelry that loves you back. Cute. They say the piano becomes an imaginary friend and alter ego wherein the artist can say everything he wants and explore his own outer limits of tenderness and wit and invention and bravado and endlessness as much as he likes. Just the same as with the perfect companion."

"While the rest of the world sits blessedly in silence."

"The other arts allow you to go back and fix things. But there's no erasing a mistake in live entertainment."

"I read where etudes are the most difficult works in the entire literature of music," he states. "I don't know that Mister Music is going to come up with any but we have set him quite a night's chore."

"Perhaps so and, you know, Host, if you think about the good old Tin Pan Alley days in New York, it was no big thing to write songs in less than fifteen minutes. Really. 'Tea for Two' was dashed off in four minutes. To be a professional song-writer you had to be able to write a tune any time, I mean, lay out a bit of melody day or night. We shouldn't be blown away if Stone can tunefully charm us all by morning."

"What kind of lyric do we suppose our priest submitted? Will it be high-brow-y or will he just pour God over everything like ketchup. Or some gaudy, musical harlotry which priests surprise us with. Like coming out."

"Ah, the unused songs of the celebate! Funny that musicians don't hate gays. Although maybe God did. Sometimes it's a case where those who shun the sex act might as well be gay, y'know. I just have to say that the Bible forbids lying with a man which would mean having sex but it does not condemn the homosexual if he keeps to himself. One can be gay without all the activity. Homosexuals merely reveal the human hurts in life that we other men dare not express." With these comments, I can discover absolutely nothing in my companion's face. Perhaps I'm going too far. Onward anyway: "Most heterosexuals don't have the genetic tragedy of impossible love. On the other hand. Straight men, we straight men are wounded from the start. We lack all built-in empathy for women, something the homosex men are perfectly instinctual about. The hetero wakens to two choices. All women must be shagged. Or. Veritably, no bitch whore will share our bed. The latter would be priests, drunks and Republicans. We machos are all physicians, making judgments on the suffering of others."

His gaze has softened. Is he gay then? Have I brought him out? What the hell, I ask about his own amours.

XXXII

"I am no *arriviste* regarding love," he offers. "Quite to the point, old chap, some time ago, I went to a crush at Lady Brandon's. As I took in the room, I was gazing at once upon the most striking, young woman I had ever seen. Her hair was an extraordinary crimson-red. She was such a vision of femininity that I was loathe to approach her even as she was in conversation with several lucky blokes. Almost at one moment, the hostess fell upon me with welcoming chatter and soon my *amour* was lost to my sight for good amid the circumlocutions of party talk." He winks at me and cocks his head as if freshly sizing me up. Then he goes on. "Well. As fate would decree, about a fortnight or so later, there I was out-country in Surrey, walking the meadows, and I actually spied her driving a dog-cart round the countryside, her red hair flying in the wind. The sight of her made my senses reel as if we had been misfortunate lovers separated as contrived by some cruel author. Then, mind you. Months later, I was chatting up a gentlemen who had attended the same Brandon social hobnob and who revealed to me he heard that a certain titian-haired beauty had expressed great disappointment at having to leave the gathering early without a chance to meet, of all people, me. Love can be so….so…inconvenient."

"We splash about quite fondly at parties, don't we, and often miss a yearning heart."

"Not to worry. I learned sometime later that she went off and married an Egyptian. All those temples and brothels and odalesques. Not to mention the whole lot over there. Palestine, Turkey, Lebanon, Djibouti."

"Yeah, may their tribes not increase."

"But you know hardly a day goes by I don't think of her, that wafting, wondering sense of reserved prettiness."

"Odd you didn't pursue her. Or were you, um. . .?"

"I was very slightly married."

"Ahhhh. The punishment for being male. And where is the Mrs. today, if I may?"

"I shall just point out that she's still in England and she sees the whole bunch of swaggering, exploring, lost-at-sea Europeans as lowlife, eager profiteers, wandering invaders always intent on introducing their superior languages, weapons, diseases and gods. She had not the slightest interest in colonial exploitation of the Americas, felt the entire adventure would better have been hushed-up. It's that British feeling of the freedom to live in the tense of one's choice. It's our penchant to equate good breeding with the right to rule." He smiles dreamily. He seems really to like his rhetorical flourish here. "But, In point of fact," he goes on, "the Missus and I have chivvied away all our better feelings for each other, a kind of finicky- - -I say, dear chap, am I becoming *recherche* here? Too much perhaps?"

"The courtroom of love," I suggest, wondering whatever shall we speak of now. The total awareness of something.

"Love." He exhales the word as if it were going to take physical shape in front of us. "The very optimism of love is so extravagant that there is no need for any brilliant insights except from the poets, of course."

"Poets are just philosphers without opinions, yes."

"Yes. Very good. There is great confidence about being capable of love. But few persons care to study love. Because everybody conceives himself to be proficient enough in the art of affection already. Of course, this satisfaction is utterly limited to one's own peculiar logic. We must fain put up with all the pettifoggery of love, that romantic something we wish we did not have to control. We want to be under its spell but only if we can remain intoxicated. The minute something goes bloody wrong which is to bring us to our senses, then to blazes with it. We try to love our inferiors but only with charity. Oh and the love of children. Beastly little chore-ridden collectives. We were all children wanting to be rid of youthful restrictions as quickly as a parent's back was turned. So we know their idea of returning our luuuuuuuv for them is their nasty, little art of waiting for our absence and evenually for our wallets and our bank balances."

I can't resist some waggishness: "The money of love then is the root of all evil?"

"I am hereby reminded that there is another kind of something horribly endemic of you Americans and that is in the form of your worship of puns. We outlanders always wonder what is the intended result of it all."

"Well it is our merry wont to———-"

"No! Don't tell me! Even in this light I can see the thought balloons forming over your head. Let's talk about trees or architecture or the art of being eighty."

"So we are the same age! You know, once you reach the magic of 80, everyone wants to carry your parcels and help you up on the curb even when you don't want to go there. And no matter you have forgotten your name or everyone else's name or your reason for being where you are in some moment, you need only declare your exact age, and the announcement will stifle all criticism, hostility or even tone of voice. Everybody is thoroughly surprised that we are still alive, that we are standing up at all. We are forgiven for all behavior and most of our opinions although no one condones our constant autobiography as recited without being questioned. We octos resemble vintage trees. The tree writes so much history of itself. All its arboreal incidents of life are featured in its limbs and branch growths and even its core. By examining it, we can determine a tree's career, its weathering, the mystery of its survival techniques. Do they not live on forever if we humans allow them to? Or nature's stormy violence cracks them as if the universe were angry with them?"

"I just read recently that the Hindu scriptures had a figure called the World Tree. It was pictured as growing downwards, its tubers rooted in the heavens and its trunk, its manifold branches pushes itself into the hungry uterus of the ground. I say! Listen to me!"

"And so many thoughts of a tree brings out the canine in me. Or out of me. I am going off to water the scenery, if it's okay."

"Right now, my dear fellow, the whole world's your *pissoir*. Do make sure about the direction of the night-wind. Tell you what, though. I'm going to check on something for a mo. A treat for us both. Keep a good thought. I shall return. Probably." He salutes with two fingers to the temple and strides toward the residence.

XXXIII

Alone to muse in the cover of night. The stars in their vast solutides. Yet whispering in the mind. Who can know the dying of the light? What mind can fathom it? The hell! One thing men can delight in. Have a wee anywhere. And when it's time, the urge becomes overwhelming. At this stage of necessity, I can only think of going right off the gazebo and into the dark. Ahhh! We all give darkness a name. Even if it's only with a strrrream. Dear me, what thoughts amid a million relievings. One of abstraction's necessary concerns are the daily duties our bodies command us to.

I love this day. I don't want it to end, and Host is keeping me attentive with talk and toddies and titillation. At least, I don't have to rouse myself as usual with my pen because now I have stopped writing. I can say I'm living in it. What a *menage* to be into. A full day's toot with these people. The horribleness of life is you can't remember much of it. All the seconds go by and you can only see them passing. And now. This moment. That who's-to-blame loop in my head. I remember one time deciding at last that I had completely figured out my drinking, moved to step outside into the night and immediately walked through the screen door.

Nature exhales its timelessness joining all personalities with a universal beckoning of sleep. Every human, evil, generous, layabout and minister pays his daily dues exactly the same as all the rest. Sleep and dreams. Love and fear put aside. Mortality momentarily conquered. Won't all humanity be ended someday and nature would produce its most fabulous sunset and the thunder would coerce the oceans with its roaring. We would stay asleep in death and the trees would frolic in the wind and the clouds would continue their endless attempt to depict the countenance of G-d. I'm so trying trying to get all this. Be eloquent and not care at the same time. Alone here in the dark is like the process of writing a story. The soul no longer waits for your mind. God's task is nature. Ours is to begin again. How to treat the sentences of the brain! Now the breeze, as if full of gossip, stirs the ambiance. Time's up.

Host may leave me out here forever. I wonder what music is Stone constructing from his fractal mess of randomness. Composing melodies! An unpursuable god. A frictionless chaos into which one can simply disappear. Meanwhile, I have lost five of my six to their slumbers. I am one with them become fugitive now. In bondage to them. And so. Our cavalier innkeeper awaits indoors for a *luxe de dieux*. My now empty glass has surely supplied excellent excess of its wicked liquid, and I gladly leave it in the gazebo. As I shuffle along a newly difficult path to the house, I wish I could put off all movement for a time. Yet. Even if unsteadily, it's on to the company of the Englishman!

I open the door to utter silence. Stone is exactly where he was, slumped down. Still at his piano.

He's either passed out or being abstracted or both, especially if creativity is really to be discovered in the subconscious. Is the kitchen my destination then?

And yes it is and there is the man fussing with some sort of fingerfood. He looks up, his expression complete nonchalance. "If you and I are to continue one more minute's drowning ourselves through the nighttide, I think a very strong espresso should top off our evening."

He eyes me, attempting discernment. "Where is that jolly traveler I was speaking to several eons ago?" he asks.

"Ug. Well, I'm no coffee drinker, so….."

"You will bless me every St. Patrick's Day when you've tasted my espresso. You'll see. Very strong. Very arousing. The quick-start catalyst for conversation. And. I didn't come right back to retrieve you from my backyard just yet. I'm putting together a few pats for us from a sushi roll just to freshen the palate, you understand."

"Wonderful! Your very name. Host. Marvelous!"

"Quite! I see you came through the den without communing with our Stone. Or did you?"

"He's all drooped over. Writing in the cosmos those unknown tunes in his head, speculating on the placement of notes. You know, the piano, when you are playing it, becomes an alter ego."

My companion puts on his antic look. "I think of jazz players, as little of their music that I get to listen to, I find their musical characters in some wild, inner world of those chaotic hallucinations. That's my take on it. Blind maunderings of a god the rest of us cannot comprehend," says he.

I hesitate on this. But after all. It's three in the morning. "'Blind maunderings!' Where'd you get that?"

"Ray Bradbury. Another one of his is 'machineries of sacrilege.' Like that one? I did suggest to our friend Stone that he compose the night away and bestow his artistry upon us noontime tomorrow," reminding me as drinkers often do.

Host pours a bombazine substance into a *demi tasse* and hands cup and saucer to me. It is menacingly hot to the tiniest edge of my upper lip but the aroma sends new hope to an addled sense. A quip sik (ohgod, here I go again) and very slowly my entire system begins to recognize and to know things like much-too-bright lighting. (Sudden illumination matters very much to the recovering psyche.) Objects are becoming easier to identify, voices are actually carrying messages and faces look favorable. A bigger swallow and the brutal, brilliant essence of the drink implodes itself minus what was always incomprehensible to me about coffee's taste. The essence of sour water. It is also something that will produce a wide-awake drunk.

Again, that hosting look. "I know you are proselityzed," he announces. Then stares. "Too much?"

"You mean the word or the drink?

"Jolly good. Shall we try some sushi, old boy? It's yellow tail, avocado, chutoro and bits of beluga."

Ohmy. The *tasse* of muddy stimulant is positively pharmaceutical. And the sight of the sushi suggests new life. Now he hands me a few samples on a dish plus wasabi and soy sauce at the ready. Um yum. The rice adheres perfectly. Don't the real Japanese chefs go to school for this? Host is eagerly awaiting my participation and so to the rations. I am scarfing down alternate shots of the little cakes and the not-quite-scalding beverage.

"Do sit," he says.

I realize I have been standing frozen in serendipity and am still loathe to disturb an iota of euphoria. But the high stools are just right and we both sit at the counter. Whatever conversation can exist while gobbling down this eclectic fare!

XXXIV

The British are expert at eating and talking all at once while completely ignoring any possibility of their listener's interest in responding. They do simultaneous speaking and masticating and recounting and salivating, and whenever they simply must pause their intake even for a few seconds to swallow, they show an uncanny knack of holding the other person in a brief but mesmerizing, silencing glare. The best movie eater/declaimer was George Sanders. He'd sniff as he chewed on and on and he'd go, "But you see, my dear,…" munch chew "there's no use expecting anything further from that gentleman so long as……." swallow inhale "the old fellow comes round tomorrow and…." Even when he wasn't at table, Sanders' voice and tone by themselves imparted a superiority that made you wonder if somehow he could like you. Eve Arden was another movie eater. She could dine and discourse through forkfuls of seafood salad and had that same ability to do the swallowing just at the right point in the sentence so as not to be interrupted, she another expert in continuous, controlled, culinary suspense.

Host is indeed doing his eating-rambling best but he's no Sanders. "I ran into another poet the other day," he says, munching on a fresh morsel. "These people are writers already so I am always instantly alert when they reveal themselves to be poetasters. I invited some email correspondence from him, and samples he sent were called 'Angry Poetry,' a delicious conceit even if he might not have a lot to say. It turned out his pieces furnished some good lines expressing his frustration at the conditions of horror and dishonor we all sit numbly through these days. Although I'm not sure whether to trust poets who never rhyme." Host holds up a hand to ensure silence, wipes his lips, produces a look of extreme self-satisfaction and continues. "Shall we carry on about our guests then? You seem to have a good handle on Hirsch. She does talk oceans of nonsense. It seems she simply lacks the power to modify her own consciousness. In her defense, patients simply want relief and all they get from psychiatrists is interpretations. She should read that Sufi poet, the one that goes: 'to fly toward a secret sky, to cause a hundred veils to fall each moment. Finally to take a step without feet.' There!" He flips his hand out, palm up. Then he pops a sushi and crushes softly, puts on a sweet smile as if remembering something.

"Rich Freeman was her Kismet-catch," is all he lets me say.

"Theirs is a match made under a bed!" he goes, overstepping my weak *bon mot*. "It's no secret that those persons the same as Hirsch without self-love see themselves as victims. And, as such, they definitely attract controlling people. Comedians, for example. Talk about controllers. These predatory performers love their authority and their importance. They want to dominate! Reign over everybody and everything everywhere. Audiences. Material. Writers. Strangers. Their families. Music volume. Food portions. Lighting. Air conditioners. Elevators. Card games. Seating arrangements. Directions. And the comedian's worst terror: Boredom. He can not suffer the conversation and information of whomever he most often meets. These are his prey, his props, too ordinary and too paltry except for their role as targets, I think our resident comic considers his ex-wife just one of his daydreams. She has to invent his version of her very self. Meanwhile, she deprives herself into some sense of mania. It's the stuff of literature, I tell you."

"But who counts as mentally ill? Who gets to determine that?" I finally come in. "What does it mean for those who get to control them? And who are those captivators? Such questions change over time as society shifts. In one age, the priests are the controlling group. In another, it's the doctors in charge. Then the media. Then the internet. Now it's just money. This has implications for how the so-called mentally ill get treated. It means that the values we think are timeless and absolute are really in constant, historical flux relative to who has power and how it gets used. You know, this synchronicity thing Hirsch is enthralled with proves that the present for her is a useless state."

"Hey! That little speech is right off the couch!" He smiles.

"Well, we can't all be psychotics. No sign of paranoia with Miss Millie-Millions, though. She's got that hardened embrace of wealthy power. I say she's a woman many men would want to love but don't think they're up to her high purposes. People like Millie should become teachers. Write a hundred times on little, blackboard minds that knowledge is the only way to make money. After all, Millie won't be defined by her glamour, or for that matter by the riches she enjoys. She has a firehouse of cash, probably enough to buy South America. Ah, I mean why do we find it so extraordinary any time a monetarily-endowed individual manages to create anything at all besides more wealth? Money can't dance forever. You have to do something with it. A teacher's treasure. And she's got it!"

"The rich worship themselves," he states.

"I say, are we going to discuss God? For that matter, I have a feeling Millie and Father could have quite a conversation concerning wealth and the Church. All about the vanishing deeds of men. Indeed there was a time when everyone believed in God, worshipped regularly and the Church ruled. We called this period the Dark Ages. Go figure. Actually, for much of its existence Christianity has been the most intolerant of world faiths."

"All men need the gods, as Homer had it. We are afraid of anything we can't explain. That's philosophy then come to help us out. Philosophy is studied so you can endure your own company, eh?"

"And the opposite of philosophy is certainty."

"Hey, we're good. Let's conclude with the notion that God is necessary if only to cause us all to fall asleep every night and, therefore, God must exist."

I rise, less wearily than I expected. "I wish someone would explain me to God."

"Maybe it's just that God's avoiding you." He's laughing. "Um. Just a bit of Anglo pettifoggery to shunt you off for the night."

I glance at the empty trays and the debris of *demitasse*, and he assures me of the necessity for slumber as he directs me from the kitchen through a small door and off to bed. "Through here," he informs me "is a small dressing-room and loo, and above it there's a loge which overlooks the garden. You'll like the lair, I'm certain. Off you go now, I need my *lebensraum*. Surely we both are sufficiently kippered in alcohol and self-discovery."

I move to embrace him. He hugs me back. In his arms for a moment, I feel existentially content, a benign, frictionless vastness into which one could simply disappear. Then, I am released and quickly out the indicated door on my way to that merciful swoon of unconciousness, mortality momentarily slumbered, to knit up the bard's old ravel'd sleeve of care. I behold the afforded space with its powder-room, everything so heavily furnished, emphasizing its smallness. But the balcony, as I ascend the little circular staircase, is all books plus sleeping quarters for one. A giant four-poster fully occupies the limited accommodation. And, wonderment! There on the nightstand wickedly sits a bottle of my Barcelona brandy, Carlos Primero, with a note that reads, "For leo J." I pick it up just to dream ahead to its pursuasions. But tomorrow's another day of searching out the characters. So, down to my shorts, I slip under the huge comforter. Such escapism is for everyone. Human need for sleep and the mystic hush of the world. My body settles. Then, that first pause of rest. I feel that someone two miles away can hear my breathing. As if in protest to this thought, the rain suddenly beats down on everything. . .falls and falters. . .and takes up again its noisy descent. All plans and purposes are nooked into safe rooms, dry and away. Am I thinking rather then writing? Am I writing? A puny habit! What indeed is the great essence of creative writing? That the world is now entirely my own idea? It tells me to abandon the center of the universe. Oh, the quality of the darkness. Where we have no destinations. And now the benighted part of staying warm begins its soporific effects.

XXXV

It's an explosion of thunder waking me up from my usual nightmare of wandering around lost in a sprawled out but well-identified city and not able to remember where my car is or anyone's phone number and can't find a telephone that works anyway. Dreams leave no hints for the sleeper. Never anything to comprehend, recalling only the fright of helplessness. Nothing the next day to validate their phantom occurrence except to tell someone anyone who will simply wonder why you need to and so you are mad about your own madness and gleeful at the same time about the freedom to have such challenges in the night that can be solved by awakening and thereby ended and no matter because suddenly they no longer exist and that happy knowledge dissolves into a new day which is not new at all just free of the horrors of the night and once more nothing becomes nothing as the new day is lost all over again. . .gone to the sense of who you are and who everyone has decided you are. No. Not yet not God or His capitalization or His insignificance when we sleep. I always try to keep up having the schema in those moments in the dream when the sleeper can realize he is alive and active the same as when awake and do as he wishes in his existence there because he knows he can totally reject the possibilities of consequence for anything he decides to do. No action he chooses to take while living in dream fantasy will be to his discredit; one can think of this idealized state that somehow he could act as he wishes. Leap over a snowbound barrier or fly in a second to another part of the ground or maybe lift the skirt of a stranger on the street although in a dream one cannot quite get to the real business of love. Time no longer governed by clocks a life on its own ohmy daylight wakes away the slumber from the good dreams as well as from the bad ones.

I am really trying to rouse completely but the covers are too heavy and when I breathe, the air is also heavy, I am reclining on my back, flat out, with my arms straight down at my sides. Like in a coffin. I have gone through the previous day and now must realize a fresh entrance into a strong, present tense. How did I fare? Sensing perhaps too keenly my putative obligations *vis-a-vis* creations now quite Pirandellian? I am allowing my characters to bring me forth. Or am I feeling too strong as in the way a writer masters his inventory of language or an actor commands center stage or the sense of privilege a preacher has from his pulpit or a docent on her museum tour? One writes with a need for relief from others all day and belonging to a world that doesn't know him and it's just being alone on the blank sheet of life and the lost pages of failure and soon the entire notion of existence is not important so long as the eyes open onto whatever hope was put to bed the night before and whywhyhow does sleep empower us more than we need just so that the soul cannot die before the body does?

A distant phone rings annoyingly through my maundering. The diabolical sound messily fuses with the alcoholic detritus of the morning. My head now has the heartbeat of an elephant. Yet I rise if only to peer out the window Host had mentioned about something involving a view of the garden. Another day's light, cruelly fabulous, punishing only me in all my bloodshot horrors. The weather has quite broken down during the night. The arriving morning brings gray clouds and a fine, cold mist. A strawberry bed just below the window is a mass of blossoms. I expect to see druids taking their places in the trees of the Host property. All creations the gifts of the Almighty. O Lord, Your continual storms, Your oceans and winds!

Now time to pop a few Daprisals to restore the marrow and let out some fresh panache, which is somehow always concealed in there.

Waiting for the click of the pills and still sitting here at the window, I can make out the soft lines of another day to infatuate me, albeit at nine AM. I see down the roadway, there's a nearby church with four, little, decorated spires and a Norman doorway that offers a grand load of moldings. Looks like rococo has suffered a decline so severe, no one remembers what the hell it means. Architecture! A demonstration of the history of human values. Some architects have quite the amount of obscure style in their prose, too. What did Balmond write? 'Architecture will always implicate the wall.' The abundant occupation of the draftsman! Compression of art into form. I always liked the Spanish architect Gaudi. This artist sexualized the very fabric of Barcelona with his many buildings and parks and arenas.

Ah, but it is time to forsake the war of words in my head. I am generally luxurious with morning ablutions but not today when my six characters are waiting with their repertory of erstwhile imaginings. Showered and dressed amd I, now it is their muffled voices possibly at a Hosted breakfast enticing me from my roost and so then what musical triumphs will Stone somehow have created during the night? He would have been hip to a sleeping society that well suits the composer. Happy the man with a good tune in his belfry! The populations of my mind now sprung to life and facing each other! The *coup de theatre* of the Author In Search Of Six Characters!

XXXVI

After a quick shower, exiting my quarters and down the stairway, I tote my Carlos Primero bottled gift. And there in the kitchen perch Millie and Priest at their breakfast and giddily engaged in table talk. *"What's the purpose of literature anyway,"* **goes one.** *Actually ,I always thought it to be a harmless oddity And I'm telling you reading's a waste of time"* **comes back the other. And,** *"It's only Darwin, don't you see? It's all-around survival that by writing you hope to attract a mate."* **I'm thinking, let it all roll.**

Host is at his forge and as I softly move to him, I gesture to his work-in-progress and speak in a lowered voice. "I see your hospitality is your never-ending life….."

He is preparing pancakes "Like some poor, little scrubber, I'm always the one who makes the tea," he says, softly.

"And how are these two characters doing?"

"They came right in around eight o'clock. Couldn't give a toss about morning edibles of any sort and got right into whatever colloguy they were born to," he sighs. "No air of formality at all. As they showed up, they even began with a light kiss, which seemed to surprise them both." He grins darkly. "No matter. I am whipping up that accident of the flame, *crepes suzette*! I've got specially brandied cherries for toppings or you can have plain ones with crisp, browned edges. My favorite! And Vermont-maple syrup." He looks determined to be full of culinary mischief all of which secret magic will probably die within.

I boorishly choose a sampling of each delicacy, tasting first the plain, under ribbons of syrup, before assessing the fruity one. The pancake edge is a crispy-crunchy delight. "So where are these two in conversation by now?" I am still *soto voce*.

"Perfectly inspired," says he. "Although they are too much *au fait* on their themes for my poor wit. I have decided on a tactful, slouchy silence. What did Shaw say? Tact is for people not witty enough for sarcasm." Their exchange now shuts ours down. Especially as they are finishing off their breakfast.

The priest is all grit and duty. His hands move in slow, episcopal gestures. And Millie is giving up her customary attention to style in favor of deep sincerity.

He's saying: "Is the world perfect or do we want to argue with God about this?"

She's saying: "God. What am I to God, really? I don't sense anything except being a murky, little shadow. My passage on earth is too rapid to leave any traces." She pauses. He nods for her to continue. "God doesn't pay any attention to our exploitations, so even if He does exist, it's as if He chooses to remain an Almighty neutral mystery, inseparable from chance. I began as Jewish as can be but in time and in certain exigencies have chosen instead to survive somehow in my own personal camouflage. At least, it keeps my moral freedom intact. God's natural disasters have killed enough of us. The old boy should observe his own Sixth Commandment about all that." She takes a swallow of her morning coffee. "Let's see now, dear priest." Finishes the cup. "Two thousand years have gone by and not a single, new god has come to us."

"Ahh, Millie," he sighs. "Man desires neither God nor Christ. He just wants the authority of the Church."

"I have confessed that I'm a secular Jewess. And if I were somehow to be a Catholic, there would be facing an impenetrable mystery how God can simultaneously be one and three. Surely you know that for Jews and others, I suppose, it is extremely difficult to ascertain whether the prayers are addressed to God or Jesus or both, whether indeed the two are identical or distinct. We have our one prophet Moses, you know, and we did not find it necessary to make him the son of God plus God Almighty at the same time. Besides, Jews disagree that any person can be called the son or the daughter of God more than any other."

"Well, miss, I agree with you in that there is confusion. How do you like that? Actually, it is that Catholics believe that Jesus, as a Jew, had no intention of establishing a new faith. Really, all the tenets of his teaching have been anticipated by the biblical prophets from six or eight centuries before his time. Even his method of teaching by parable was charcteristic of Jewish pedagogy. He was a critic of much in Judaism that warranted disaccord in his time, following the precedent of Moses, Amos, Isaiah and Jeremiah. You with me here?"

"Goodness, Father, you know more about my old religion than I do."

"That's the irony, dear lady. You're the fallen Jew, while I the Catholic think no one can be Christian without being Jewish as well. The Jews more than any other people have shown an exceptional capacity to inquire into the cosmic meaning of the human experience. And." He takes a breath. "To distill from that significance, a code of ethical standards by which all can become most truly human. Shall I go on? I can be sometimes too grasped by faith." We all three murmur encouragement as his spiritual enlargement intensifies. "All right. Jesus had a method of propounding by parable which was characteristic of Jewish pedagogy. There was, indeed, much at the time to warrant his criticism. But Jesus was following his Jewish predecessors. You know," he sips, "if Jesus returned to earth, he would be much more comfortable in a synagogue than in a church. The cornerstone of Judaism was the deed, not the dogma. Different strokes for us guys, however. The fundamental characterictic of Christianity, as it was preached by the apostles, and as it is embodied today contemplates one thing only: unconditional and steadfast faith in a person; that person being, of course, the founder. Believe in the lord Jesus and thou shalt be saved. We know Christian and Jew appealed to different sides of human nature, the former to the passive side, the latter to the active side. Christianity stressed faith, Judaism, proper action. Our side had to keep our faithful in line by our thunderous sermons showered upon the peasants to shock them into virtue and frighten them into heaven. Such dark vocabulary engraves itself so very deeply."

We applaud him lightly. He feigns surprise.

"It's the crucifixion that gets everybody going," Millie entering in. "Did the Jews murder the savior! Blame the unbelievers! But the landscape of Judea was filled up with plenty of Roman crosses and Jewish bodies hanging from them. Jesus being crucified was not unique. He was one of tens of thousands of Jewish political victims of Rome whenever the rulers got challenged. And then the absolute *chutzpa* of it all. The early church needed converts and, therefore, mentioning—not to say, glorifying—such a horrible death was not cool. It took a long time to admit things, it seems, and finally the crucifixion was only slowly made important by art. Yeah!"

"The Bible unfortunately doesn't teach you tolerance," asserts the priest. "You go there for passion, for zealousness, for extremes. Those biblical characters were all Jacobins, radicals, Miss

Millie, and their passions instill all that religious fervor for one's own beliefs while excluding those who do not share those beliefs. You know the calumny against the Jews has been apologized for and condemned. I am sad to say there are still many anti-Semitic Christians for whom there is no distinction whatsoever between the Jews of two thousand years ago and those of our day. This is quite the absolutely wretched defamation which holds that a prosperous minority deserves constant scorn."

Millie: "If God exists, He certainly designed us for trouble. And how about this last great day stuff? You mickeys—excuse me—you, uh…."

"Go ahead." He's laughing. "We can take it."

"You guys have this religious premise from one of your books——"

"Revelation. I know where you"re going."

"—describing the scenario of the end of the world. See if I have this," she says. "When the messiah returns, true believers will be lifted into heaven where, with God, they will get to observe the torture of the unlucky ones, the other humans who are left behind. This transcendent event will be instantaneous and the timing, unpredictable. How'my doin' so far? And true believers will suddenly be whisked away to heaven. And this brings in the role of Israel, the desire of the world. Everyone wants to posess her. She must not be taken by force for her Father is very jealous and He never sleeps but that's why so many evangelicals support Israel because it's the place they're really going to need to still exist when the time comes. The Israelites' return to the promised land was a requirement of the second coming, right? Meaning the role of the nation of Israel at the denouement of history. I'm done."

"You're talking about the Baptists, dearie. We mickeys believe all the good will go to heaven and the bad won't make it and they'll be all by themselves and left with their evilness somewhere dark and awful. To take over the pulpit for a moment, I would point out that the book of Revelation is an example of apocalyptic scriptural literature. As such, it is not to be taken literally as Christian fundamentalists do but rather, figuratively. Or, more precisely, metaphorically. The author of the Book of Revelation, supposedly St. John, was writing in very vivid, you could even say, frightening terms to capture the attention of people. Another thing. At the time of these tidings, it was commonly believed that the end of the world would be very soon. Very. That is, within—get this—within the lifespan of the people who were indeed living at that time."

XXXVII

A pause is upon us. Host is saying, "All these salty lucubrations may require more fuel. Fresh cakes, anyone?"

"A controversial moment in the history of thought," goes Father, "but let's get back to God. I am more comfortable just relying on the Almighty where there is endless spiritual nourishment."

"We fail God by worshipping ourselves." Millie keeps on. "That's how I found belief to be incompatible. I realized the mind is nothing but a darkroom with an audience of one. Me."

"I'm always surprised when I learn that someone has given up her Judaism. These biblical souls have somehow been able to maintain a deep attachment to their literature which spells out the ultimate mandate for those who must demonstrate the presence of God to the world. And the Chrisitians waste their spiritual time going on and further onward about their life after death and thus reducing the value of their time on earth. The Jews always toast 'to life' in that the here and now is priceless compared to the great infinity of death. Christianity has made of death nothing but a gruesome comedy, a perversion of all values."

"I don't need a religion for that," she says. "I only wish someone's god would help me make it on my own. Can yours do that?"

"Read your Torah then."

"Sorry. It's all about righteousness. There's not a word of metaphysics in the Bible. HIstory, yes, and laws, prophecies, proverbs, poems. And stories. Very little that is abstract and speculative, nothing like the Greek aesthetics or Indian philosophy of the same period. Jewish prophets are quite reticient when it comes to saying what God is truly like."

"I must say that having a faith is a confidential process, Miss Millie, known only to each adherent.

And this secret cannot be articulated. It amounts to facing sacred moments."

"I can say, parson, that in taking over Judaism, you Christians have confused the issue with so many new angels, miracles and hallucinations that the worldly significance of monotheism—not to mention democracy—all but vanished. And, say, do you think God has pardoned the Catholics for giving up Latin? I don't even think He's forgiven the Latinos for giving up the bossa nova."

The Reverend laughs heartily at this remark. "Eve the woman, oh ha ha, the, the woman, ho, she tastes of the apple and, ha ha, once the sacred giver of life, she is now the enemy. You *are* funny! Death and all his hideous train are at my heels for all this heresy," he announces in a biblical basso.

"Better a heretic than an apostate," she intones, her voice attempting to emulate the portent of the prelate. "Civilization," she continues, "will not attain perfection until the last stone from the last church falls on the last priest,"

"But, see," he goes. "every society must have a religion to give authority to its cultural practices. It causes a harmony with our social ethos. And one can be an atheist and still be a Jew, don't you think? Surely one definition of Jewishness goes beyond just Judaism. That the religion is a social force, one that must include all Jews, not just those who participate most fully. All the traits of nationhood, language, literature, history, culture, destiny, stop me."

"Ah, the clouds and phantasms of religion. But how the hell could the church claim that Jesus was universally divine if his own people disclaimed him?"

"Read your Jewish-Greek Philo for that one. He suggested that God's very first creation was not heaven and earth but reason and intelligence."

"But I say God created an intelligent creature cursed never to understand Himself. Or. OR! God was a neurotic who created man so that God could understand Himself. Is it time for cocktails yet?" she glances away.

"Maybe it's just that God's willing to wait for you," says the priest, and this as Freeman enters.

"I see I've missed all the social anxiety," is his *non sequiter* but he goes silent at the coffeepot in the corner.

Millie smiles a very beguiling glance at him, unusual for her. He doesn't see it. Then he does. Almost spits his beverage. She says, "Where was I?"

The Father: "If everybody in the world wants to, we can just reduce the essence of all religion to a common, vague and harmless and numinous ambience with which even the unbeliever can decorate his own outlook. I realize that we are struggling with abstractions. It does nothing but excuse our endeavors and blind us to our failures. Besides, religion outside the church is annoying. Or did I already say that? And I admit that what the

Christian church offers me most is an eternity of frustration."

"Can it be one's sexual energy is lost to clerical culture?" A poorly-veiled inquiry from me.

"Becoming a flaming neuter is not a big deal. I'm as celibate as fifty percent of American women. And, what the hey, non-indulgence is no root canal. It is painless, free and convenient. Talk about safe sex! You don't have to do anything afterwards like try to be nice to anybody because there is no afterward, and when my TV is flashing boobs, et cetera, I go get a beer. You know, the vow of abstinence was put in place originally because the church did not want clergy having any heirs making claims on money and land. But it ended up shrinking—if I may use the word—diminishing the priestly pool and producing the wrong kind of candidates, bringing in men confused about their sexuality who disgrace the cloth by putting our children in harm's way. You could also say that Catholic schools and their corporal punishment for students relieved the monks of the strains of self-denial. For me, the higher vocation of celebacy was far better than the consolation prize of marriage. One can also be blissfully gay without all the activity."

"And the nuns were safe if all the men were third sex." It's Freeman as he munches on something.

All but priest make a face at him and the cleric waves his indifference. "No offense. There was no more imperial partriarchy than was the church.

Nuns were second class citizens for sure and today, fifty years after feminism utterly changed America, the sisters are still not considered equal in contribution, spirituality and, worst of all, the capacity to nurture. The concept of women as priests is a forbidden topic, believe me. The Cardinal who would become Benedict XVI wrote a Vatican document urging women to be submissive and to resist even in their innocent hearts any adversarial role with men. They were to cultivate feminine values like listening, welcoming, humility, faithfulness and, heaven-help-me, waiting. This life sentence from a pope who was christened God's rottweiler for his enforcement of such orthodoxy!"

Millie: "Brides of Christ should sue for divorce."

"They probably wouldn't be around for any settlement as nuns are a dwindling group with an average age of about 70. The Vatican, in expunging any speck of modernity or independence, will wipe out the entire holy contingent. It is easy to observe the church enabling rampant pedophilia while, at the same time, nuns who live in apartments and do social work with ailing gays are denounced as sacrilegious. This is why, madam, that I love your former religion. Judaism, in freeing itself, also frees humanity from bondage. And in the process into a rich life of introspection. It helps God in his search for mankind."

She puts her cup aside. "God, you say? All his created humanity will end anyway when nourishment runs out, when billions of people are more than the planet can sustain."

"What then?" says Doll. She has come in from the outside. She is a miracle of bright, malicious humor all ready for discovery.

XXXVIII

"Nature will do her thing," continues Millie, suddenly brightening at the presence of another female. "On the so-called last great day, nature will create its most extravagant twilight and the mountains stay asleep—I am paraphrasing the Union Prayer Book."

"You're right," goes Doll. "It's very strange, you know, but sometimes I can spot the face of God shaped in the clouds."

"What's He look like?" is Freeman.

"I donno. An old, wise man, I guess. Just his head. Something like Edmund Gwenn maybe."

The priest: "We must rely on the God we identify whether in the heavens or in our hearts or our prayers. Even if He does not correspond to any of our rational categories. We believers are always at prayer even if we don't perceive it. The subconscious is in constant petition either for relief or for gain or just feeling gratitude for good fortune. We're constantly saying 'thank God' in resonse to just anything. Or prayerful judging ourselves in endless pursuit of justification. That's the truth of faith."

I try: "Which is easier to understand? Truth, as you mention it, or art?"

Millie: "Which is easier to forget, say I!"

Doll does: "Truth is, men punish us because they can't be the same as us. No, they can't!" She's coolly trying again to change the subject. "The one world males want us to see is whatever we can think up while we are on our backs. The best art for a woman is to use the male's desires as our weapon against his enslavement. "

"You are right," cheers Millie. " We women defend ourselves very easily. We attack by sudden and strange surrenders."

The men are stricken dumb. All eyes are dull as if we've just been told that all drinking-alcohol in the world has suddenly and mysteriously turned into cider.

"There is a generation," Millie begins, "that is growing up around us that by-passes the church to find its worship in the art galleries, the movie houses and rock shows. This cultural explosion is a general revulsion regarding secular materialism. And if that's too *outre*, then let's just say the kids hate hypocrisy and they hate boredom. Religions today are nothing more than simple repetition. Many a person enters a church only for viewing the stained glass brilliance of a Chagall. You know what? I think God is actually against art."

"Aren't you going to discuss Islam?" This is Freeman from his corner.

"You first," says Millie to the priest.

"Well, Muslims want both stagnation and power. A return to the perfections of the seventh century and still be able to dominate the twenty-first. They believe that their birthright is the doctrine of taking over the world. It began with a vision in a cave or an angel on the horizon but today the adherents are determined to show no impotence before the West and all its triumphant secularism. Their traditions have been swamped by the prominent Judeo-Christian culture."

I chime in: "Yes, Islam is not going to disappear or wither away. But about American *Mooslims*, so very far away from the prophet Mohammed's dictum that this ancient man's religionists should primarily cloak themselves in the virtues of compassion and generosity. They were imbued to use their intelligence to cultivate a caring and responsible *elan*, thus to acquire a spiritual refinement. And they never seem to blame themselves. It's always the rest of us corrupting the world they suppose they own somehow. What their American adherents need is they should be subjected to experiencing a period of living under serious, Islamist rule and they would soon grasp the foolish parts of the religion they live in."

"They should discover that wonderful luxury about self-reproach," says Millie. "When we blame ourselves, we feel instantly that no one else therefore has any right to blame us."

"And a fine bunch you are, here to give up your scripturgiac addiction to writing and transcend this everyday world and generate philosophy, theology and art, and, uh, well, what have we discovered?" comes Host. "Anyone?"

"That the Crusades, the Inquisition, the witch hunts, slavery in America, child sexual abuse and the Iraq war are hardly ideals of Western civilization, as propounded from Christian values," says Millie

"That I suddenly know why God decreed prayer and fasting because the saddest prayers are the ones asking for food," says the priest.

"That really the only available god is the computer," says Freeman.

"That all literature causes me to sigh," says Doll.

"That inactivity is better than mindless function," says Hirsch. The sleepy-headed woman has entered and is immediately responding in tandem with the others. She goes over and takes deep swallows of orange juice that Host puts before her.

"The healing power of candor," says Freeman, observing her.

Hirsch looks up with cheeks puffed full of liquid. She swallows. "Talent is developed in privacy. There is a need for aloneness which most people don't realize. I wish some artist would paint me out." She screws up her face, draws her eyes together and makes her mouth small and tight. No one speaks. She looks around at everybody. "Butterflies to a flame," she says. Can she be channeling Dorothy Parker? "Maybe we need to write a play for ourselves to appear in. Call it 'Backing into the limelight.' Host could play the butler."

She waves him off with his immediately proferred pitcher of juice. "How's Stone doing with all your lyrics?" She's still on. "Where is he anyway? It's going to be brilliant, I tell you. I once had a spark of jazziness when Freeman and I were in New York on 52nd Street. The trio in the bar, playing the date, was Red Norvo, Tal Farlow and Mingus, and they were doing an arranged, combined sound very in vogue at the time. The vibraphone was in block chords with the guitar doing the melody in tandem and after a few minutes, I said loud enough, 'Who needs Shearing!!' and the audience all laughed. The band didn't though. Jazz is so unpredictable. Like an unexpected climax."

"Women can fake even multiple orgasms," offers Doll, trying to lighten the other woman's mood. "But men can fake entire relationships."

"It's all synchronous proving again that the present moment is useless," says Hirsch.

Priest and Millie stand up as if in silent accord.

"Well, Miss Millions. Ooops! I didn't mean that, Millie." He bestows a broad smile.

"I got it," she laughs. "You wanna talk about the almighty dollar. The one thing ruining our democracy is the idea that rich people need to get more money. What were we about to say?"

"I was going to suggest that you and I check out the power of landscape before Stone begins pelting us with tunes." He grins at Millie. "Let's take a little post-prandial stroll outdoors if it's stopped raining."

They approach the exit to the garden. She is asking, "Shall we talk theology or philosophy?"

Father has a look of holiness, the one expression priests practice when they are not so good at disseminating revelation. He takes Millie by the arm and they exit through the doorway with Millie telling him, "You say God is necessary and so must exist but I know he......"

XXXIX

"Those two will find their burdens again. Priests get so bored with nothing to feel but guilt, and secular Jews are bored with nothing in their life but freedom," offers Freeman.

Host gets up from his culinary speculations. "Now I must see to Stone. He's been up all night, I would think, and perhaps we'll all become famous for his melodies." He exits into the library, and so, Freeman with no one left but Doll and yours truly as his game, announces out of the side of his mouth to me: "Get my swan costume ready."

Doll shows no sign of hearing this but yet, knowing her. . .

"Are you famous?" She wastes no time starting on the comic.

"Yes," says he. "One of the great wonders of our stage is the curse of deciding to be a comedian. Of course, to not be one is even worse. I am a microphone. Everyone else is a hearing aid."

"I was promoting a movie once in London," she says, calmly, "and Lawrence Olivier was somewhere in town performing and I snuck inside the stage door and, unnoticed, wandered to his dressing room."

Freeman is mum at this news as she goes on.

"I tapped on the door and waited a few seconds and then pushed and walked in and there he was. O. LIV. VEE. YAY. I saw him staring at the wall, holding a tumbler in his hand. Face still black from the Shakespeare." She acts as if she expects Freeman to say something but nothing comes out of him. "Well, anyway, he never looked at me and so I got kinda jittery to think where the hell I was. Here am I standing next to this major movie star, and you know in the porno movies, I was always the vamp, managing to get the plot going. I would expect to die in bed but certainly not in my own bed. So Lawrence Olivier never spoke or cared or noticed. Anyway, I felt like a dancehall girl or something but I just got the hell out of there."

Freeman looks at me. "It's the decline and fall of practically everybody."

"Will Cuppy," I suggest.

He lifts both palms up. "I feel like someone is drawing a chalk line out on a sidewalk somewhere and it's shaped like me. Is it too early for a drink?" he says to the ceiling.

"The consumption of alcohol may cause pregnancy," she goes on.

He tries: "My conscience is always immediately soluable in alcohol."

And she: "I don't know if I like alcoholics anyway. They never call you when YOU"RE drunk."

For a few seconds, he puts on a what-the-hell face. "You remind me of the time a hooker told me she had a headache."

"Listen, I played so many movie vamps, they'd just leave my pay on the dresser."

HIrsch is still sitting there. "This man was a major comedian which is to say that he had the compassion of a carnival shill and the generosity of a pawn broker." She's up and toward the den door. "I'm going in to the loo and putting my coat over my head." Gone.

Doll stares at the door Hirsch has left ajar. "Do you two know if it is ever time to forgive? You both share such a good sense of distaste."

"It's life," he goes. "Life tells you when to forgive. It's always somewhere in hell."

"Too bad you didn't find your way to a little risk-free sexuality."

"What the christ are we talking about?"

"Okay. Here," she says. "Two cows are standing in the pasture. One turns to the other and says——-" she effects a deep and ridiculous baritone which sound alone is enough to make me laugh out loud. "Although the designation 'pi' is abbreviated to five numbers, it actually goes on into infinity'. The second cow turns to the first and says, 'MOOOO'." She giggles. "Pretty good for a blonde, huh?"

Freeman counters: "The attorney asks the blond witness, 'Are you sexually active?' And she says, 'No, I just lie there.'"

"Hey, you're a goddam professional comic so the least thing about you is you're gonna be funnier than me but I don't want to hang around with somebody who will end up outside my window hollerin' for me to at least throw his pants out the window."

"Let's park it," he suggests. "Storman here can referee." They sit at the counter. I offer to mix together a few screwdrivers for them.

"What's the most favorite place you've ever been," he starts with.

"My favorite? Ohwell, the Crossroads Inn, I would say."

"God. Another woman destroying me. So you've actually been in love?"

"If I know anything about love, at least I can state I am not in love now. I remember Rita Hayworth saying, 'They go bed with Gilda and wake up with me.' And if you want to know about myself, you have to look at the porno flicks. I went by the name of Doris ClitORus."

Jesus, I'm thinking. Yegods. What a dame. Talk about having a fertile crescent.

It's Freeman. "Hey, do the chicks in the F-films have actual orgasms? Men so want them to."

"Well, you know, sometimes it's written in the contract that the female coming attraction better be real. It didn't matter to me. Although. Sometimes a good rapture just pops out. Like loose dentures." She nods at me as I place the vodka mixture before her.

Then the cocktail for him. "The war of words goes platinum," I mutter.

She studies his face intently. "You! Are a wet-dream waiting to happen!"

"Well, I'm positioned on your one-yard line. Let's see what I'm going to call."

"Yeah. That's what kills me about you, Freeman. Why does your ex-wife want to bother with your ass?

"You ever heard about love without fun? That's her. She thinks I'm Santa Claus."

"You know, this is no kidding," she says. "I read where Shirley Temple actually said she stopped believing in Santa Claus when she was six. Her mother took her to see him in a department store and when she got up on his lap, he asked for her autograph. Anyway, what does HIrsch know about loving a man like you?"

"Many a wife thinks her husband is the world's greatest lover but she can never manage to catch him at it. No, seriously. She showed me a report from one of her virtuoso therapists. And—this is deep—but it stated that life for her is either a mirror or a window. One is in which she sees herself backwards or the other one revealing or, say, framing the world to look out upon but not be a part of. You know? Either it's a contant reflection on yourself or that all the world is always someplace else. Heavy, yes? But it's all her power poured into emptiness."

"You do like to hide yourself in word inventory," she suggests. "But surely Hirsch gets tired of being a person with a line drawn through her name."

XL

This duet of wit and wench is noisily intruded upon with the re-appearance of Millie and Priest as she is heard, "I got myself involved in one long righteous improv with this prelate. It ended when we actually agreed that people can be good without God. And what else. Yeah, that saints are often just fanatics and dangerous. And, and I pointed out to him there are very few secular laws demanding good acts. Think of it, I told him. Almost no secular laws demanding good behavior. The only one we have is a law that makes criminals do community service. We force them, force felons to help others. It's not a joy for them. Caring for others is a punishment."

She tries a sly look at the orange juice. And waves a forefinger up-and-down at the vodka bottle on the counter. I hop into service. She continues with no regard for the potentiality of the on-going conversation of others. "And where are we anyway? Six characters caught in some narrative register so we can become fugitives from the art of writing?!" She gulps down some potation. "And is it also indeed some elegant illusion that we can live another life!"

"Yes," says Father, with strong portent on his way to the fridge for a beer. He twists it open and gulps. "We always tear our gods to bits, don't we? Especially when we're writing. Composition of any kind, scribbling, scrawling, the calisthenics of words. We must treat sentences as objects found on the beach. Non-treasures. Tossed and gone."

"I like this pastor." she emotes. "Our high-voltage messiah is the lucky one here. He flows so easily from literature to religion. It's almost musical! And religion is an art, too, isn't it? And, of all the arts, then, really, religion has the most prestige because everybody can claim he's into it. No talent required, eh?"

"How true," priest says, "We writers are the same as those sad, captive nuns in Catholic custody. Writers and nuns deal with imperfection. That's what we go on about. Instability." He makes an appealing gesture with both hands. "We'll all be cured now, Host, won't we?" He glances about for an absent caretaker. "Where can he be? Checking out Stone, I suppose." He examines his palms for a moment. "I hope he's all right. I wouldn't want to be giving him last rites for his last wrongs. Ah, how precious is the anticipation of musical immortality. It's positively priestly." He smiles at Millie for response.

She looks pleased to speak. "I like you clerics most when you are content to be something in jewelry or chocolate. But. Alas. I am constrained to make as much money as I can. Banks love me. No place for a priest, right, Father?"

"You know, there is a reason banks are made to look like temples because long before the government got into the act, commerce was rooted in ancient moral codes, not just in market indices and interest rates. Anyway, we clerics don't have to bother with money so that we can spend our time explaining demise. Somehow the priesthood never tires of assuring people about death and its handmaiden, the horror of waiting. If there is something worse than despair, it's the waiting. We pulpiteers try to instill in our laity the ability to linger."

So these two gamecocks are still at it! "There's not one word in the Gospels in praise of having brains either," she posits. "God's nothing but a control freak, I tell you." She smiles. "The sssssecret of religion….." she has hissed the word 'secret' "…..is the absolute terror of God! Meanwhile," she gazes at nothing, "life has turned good for American Jews and their mistresses."

"Well said," is the priest. "After all, the very first statement that God makes about human nature is that it's not good for us to be alone. Do we pray in the howling storm or rejoice in the stars?

Hirsch has come back in. She's wearing vampy, red nail-polish and her hair elaborately twisted. "Nice mob you've got here," she growls. "I hope I'm not intruding." Now she beams an unbelievable-superior-tolerating-radiant-Malvolio smile. "We're all mingling now. Am I still real?"

I move to her side as I speak. "Why not make what we can of love? It's what we want for ourselves, isn't it? We've everyone of us suffered through too many funerals and heard how eloquently the dead are praised and threw their lives away." I am trying to figure out where my own statements are going.

"Then why does Virginia Woolf keep speaking to me?" she utters in a furious whisper.

"How about some of Host's flapjacks," proposes Millie, concerned for the tone.

"I'm on the cardiologists' diet. If it tastes good, spit it out." Hirsch recovering. She looks around for amused approval and gets it. Even from Freeman. And at this moment, she's giving it to the deciduous six, now including me in that Stone is off-stage. She hoists the nearest glass, which happens to be empty. "A toast to the death of writing," she posits.

We all raise our glasses in expectation and, as we wait glumly, it is Freeman who shambles over to the orange-juice blend and lifts it up to fill her goblet.

"*L'chayim*," snaps the priest, and all lustily consume every drop.

It is at this moment that Stone and Host enter our presence from the composer's room, as it were. Stone carries a large sheaf of music. He sees the line-up and announces, "You dudes should be aware of something. That alcohol confers only a temporary nonactivity upon the psyche. It's hallucinogens that show you the Promised Land."

Millie and Priest exchange beautific smiles at this.

"Alcohol is the same as jazz," tries Freeman. "They're both a search for another reality, right?"

"There's no longer a god even for drunkards," sniffs Millie. "Is there a god for jazz?"

"'Probably Louie," says Stone, "but my choice is Tatum."

"Art Tatum never composed a single tune," comes Freeman. "What do you make of that?"

Stone lays his musical treasures on the counter and pours some orange juice from a bottle. "Tatum was beautiful. He invented bop long before Diz or Bird and Miles. He was doing flatted fifths and syncopated riffs way past what Bud Powell one day came up with. And when Art Tatum sat in, they always gave him an extra solo. He knows other people's music better than they do and he never wrote a note because he didn't have to. He just wanted to take all the great songs and demolish them with arpeggios and crazy-chorded embroideries and counterpoint and put 'em back together again. He heard beauty everywhere. All people in the world should be like jazz musicians when they're jammin 'cause improvisation means everybody has an equal freedom to be creative but always in chorus with the others. It's the respect, man."

"Mister, uh, Stone tells me he has composed the music for our little lyrical promptings," begins Host. "And we shall ask him now to tell us about it and then, perform for us?"

"Let the songs begin!" declares Hirsch, raising another empty glass she's picked up.

S pops a J into his mouth but doesn't light it. "I have been drug-depriving myself all night into some semblance of genesis. Doin' songs for people is not like you're winging it at a session somewhere where you're just following those giant, retreating melody lines toward some version of cool. I always approach the keys like I sit down on the stool and I open the lid and with myself now in the mix, the piano begins to disclose its lower jaw so that I can bop up and down all those teeth. And there's that immediate itch in the fingers." He looks forcefully at Hirsch who slips over to him and neatly stacks and taps his sheet music.

Stone moves to the garden door. "I will be with marijane for a few moments outside, and as Kerouac often said, 'I'll be coming back - if not, then you won't see me'." He exits. The door slowly closes.

XLI

"There is nothing more exciting than to put a note of music above a word," says Freeman.

"If he can play in his condition, even the piano must be astonished," offers Millie.

"You know, in the movies, nobody needed to practice or learn any music," says Doll. "Like the musical comedies where the girl walks into the room and the boy is seated at the piano. He would go, 'Gee, Mary. Would you listen to this tune I just wrote', and the girl would stand behind him and read over his shoulder and then begin to sing it from the fifth bar on with every word in the lyric and every note in the melody perfectly rendered."

"And on the second chorus, the violins join in and the guy at the piano suddenly sounds like he's Oscar Levant."

"I also love it in the flicks when whatever movie is showing on the people's TV is far better than the movie you're watching."

"And, and, the television news bulletins immediately contain a report that directly affects the people personally the minute they turn on the set."

This is the characters all talking. I can't tell who it is at one moment. Writers are always interested in cinema, though. Really, any decent author has a life that would make an okay screenplay.

"Dietrich and Garbo modeled with such transgressive chic." They go on.

"How about Jean Harlow? I heard her number was listed in the yellow pages. And, uh, when Lana Turner wore her tight cashmere in 'They Won't Forget'."

"And Frankenstein's Elsa Lanchester with those electrocuted waves of hair."

"And Karloff carried so many bodies upstairs."

"It was always Lugosi for me," say I. "The colossal egotism and sentimentality of the vampire."

"Dunt be afrrraid," intones Freeman. "I am Drawcula and I bid you wellucum to my howss. Come in! Come in! The night air isss chill. You mussst be tyurred from your long chourney."

Light applause. Doll chimes in. "I was in a movie once called 'Vampire Hookers'. It takes place in one of those bars where everything in the air around you burns your eyes and the music is so loud you lose all your resistance."

"Funny for me were the cinema drinking parlors," goes the priest. "I loved the cowboy saloons with their orderly menace. All in the worn, raw faces of the barflies and the deadly serious expressions of the card-players with something going to explode any minute." He glances around.

Looks right now that everybody's throwing in a cinememory.

"I liked all those needy-ladydrunks. You know, Lee Remick in 'Days of Wine and Roses' or Piper Laurie in anything. Or Mercedes McCambridge and Maureen Stapleton, inebriates forever. Anybody else?"

"Yes. Why didn't Tarzan have a beard?"

"And how about Brando when they asked him what he was rebelling against and he said, 'Whaddaya got!'."

"And Edward G in 'Key Largo' with his cigar in his mouth, and when they asked him what's the one thing he wanted in life, he scowled out, 'More!'"

"How about Glenn Close when she turns vicious on the married, cheating Michael Douglas, and she screams in his face, "I will not be ignored!"

"Sex is like meeting God without dying, Dorothy Parker once remarked."

"Orson Welles said, 'I'll be remembered because I was a parade'."

"How about you, Host?" say I.

"My opinion on screen acting? Luck can teach you the works in two hours."

"This nickelodeon mood we're all in must end in music whatever Stone has for us," says Freeman. "And before he gets started, I need to tell you all that last night while you folks were blissfully abed, I played and sang my own, original Monster Song just to entertain our leo J. Storman here." He gestures to me. "And I invite you all into the music room to hear it. So. leo J. Mysterious moniker it is. Would you check outside and bring our composer indoors to play what he may from all our lyrical suggestions? By the way. What's the 'J' for?"

"Ah so." I effect a Charlie Chan touch. "Confucious say, 'Some things much clearer when looked at backwards'," with intended inscrutability as I go out to fetch The Man.

XLII

Outdoors. The afternoon world is a pleasure for me. I stand in the sunlight, gazing at the sky for a moment. A day of patternless clouds, their polymorphic randomness. Clouds are not spheres, mountains are not cones and bark is not smooth. Coastlines, lightning-jaggedness, whirlpool outlines. Fractals.

Ah, but there, seated off in the pavilion is Stone, languid, intent on smoking his joint. Amid his usual jamboree of images, one supposes.

"Go Stone-Man!" I call, as I walk towards him.

He sees me. "S;t;a;y c;o;o;l. J;a;c;k," he r;u;m;b;l;e;s. words g;r;o;w;l;e;d away g;n;a;r;l;e;d out. Then, recovering, he goes: "Did you know speed kills color? The gyroscope, when turning at full tilt, shows up gray." I can only stare at him.

Something fills his gaze, however, with a suggestion of caprice. "Most people need a glass navel to see where they are going," he gloats.

"They're all waiting for your melodies," I suggest. "The air inside is absolutely soaked in the conviction that you just love your journey from piano to piano.

He stares into my eyes. "When I am blitzed, I actually believe the keys are in the shape of breasts."

"Well, wow! Who wouldn't want to get started right away playing something?" as I step closer to him.

It seems, from the oddity of his speech that I should assist him up physically but he easily rises, takes a deep hit and flips away his smoke.

"This has become a place for my braln to work its chore."

He begins walking toward the house and, as I follow, I hear him saying, "Do you know the difference between a blues musician and a jazz musician?"

"What?" I go.

He stops, turns to me. "A blues musician plays three chords in front of a thousand people. A jazz musician plays a thousand chords in front of three people." He winks hugely, points a gun-shaped hand at me, whirls himself about and proceeds toward the residence.

He reaches the entrance. I tell him, "It's time to see if you've made any new friends."

XLIII

Who knows if Stone hears me as he enters just ahead into the melange of conversation within. I hear Host's greeting. "Ah, our maestro! You have looked out at the beacons of immortality and now a triumphant return to your leisured audience."

Hirsch comes over to Stone and they move to the piano. We all sit quietly and attentively about the room. Me next to Freeman. She holds his clutter of canticles, places all before the musician and, after a long zen moment, she arises and begins. "It is with a sense of wonder and awe that we can enjoy the creative artist at such an extraordinary time. Maestro Stone here will sing his own musical compositions as he has, I am sure, skillfully transformed you-all's lyrics to a superior place." She now seems very protective of the pianist before he's even begun.

Freeman whispers to me, "Shakespeare always knocked off the people who couldn't sing."

Hirsch wheels on him, her icycles burning. "I heard that! I can see that brain of yours beginning to silt!"

her mouth humorless and unembarrassable. "I was married to Freeman long enough to get scared at night," she goes. "We are totally mismatched; I'm a gemini, he's a whore."

"Am I becoming more mellow," cracks Freeman, "or is she just now getting funnier?"

They all chip in:

"There is some vague apprehension here that something unnamable is moving towards us."....Millie

"I feel like I'm in the Society To Prevent People From Being Creative."....Priest

"The only person I ever made happy was her divorce lawyer."....Freeman

"Me, I can't fall in love; it just seems like fiction anymore."....Doll

"The war of words goes platinum," I murmer to Freeman.

HIrsch now has the face people put on when they are addressing children. A mind amply furnished with authority. "Game on!" she suddenly shouts. "We should begin our song-feste with our proprietor Mister Host's contribution." Gestures to Stone. "Maestro, please!" She sits at the edge of the piano seat next to him.

The pianist's hands go wild, spiders on acid scrambling and stretching, searching, planting

crunching chords, burning out combinations and then, fingers of each hand starting far apart on the keyboard and rushing via the notes to meet in the center and slip smoothly into a simple, charming beginning for our dear host's lyric. Now the piano-style lightly mimics the English-pub empresarios with rolling right-hand octaves and Fats Waller stride on the left.

He begins to sing in a Stanley Holloway voice:

'Pay me in pounds
Tie me in naughts
I'll stay abovegrounds
As the brain slowly rots

Hold back the hounds
<Hirsch emits a yip of a farcical bark>

Then have afterthoughts
<pianist vamps to another key half a step up>

Now I'm reading too much
gone all literary strictures

Of course, there is the other crutch
I see all motion pictures!"

The gang love it, applaud lustily, as Stone instrumentalizes through another chorus and then a third as Hirsch reads from the script and directs, mouthing the words for them. Further cheering as Host bows an outstretched palm to the composer. Stone still very lightly vamps along while Hirsch

sets up the next number. She must have conferred with him on the musical docket as she very formally stands before us. "I feel my own song would be next as I am the only non-scripturgiac present." She arranges the page Stone has prepared for her contribution, and he segues into a mysterioso motif, minor thumping and fantasmical rhythm.

Rather than sing, he speaks her contributed lines over the beat and within the meter.

He tries a little Karloff on the vowels:

"To meet my madness
in the bawthroom mirror"

[beat, beat beat, beat]

"makes breakfast and plaidness
all sooo much dearuh."
<The music signals a deft chord change and slows down the beat.>

Stone recites on:

"Lost time gets even worse
after good times disappear."

Nature's coinage reimburse
with every falling tear."

Stone modulates into yet another key and changes his style of playing into a rag-time rhythm, much like that of his own contribution and then does the entire number again to the new, up-beat rendition. Then an exaggerated, churchy two-chord ending: "awww——-men."

"Bloody good," says Host over the easy applause.

Stone keeps the music cascading as he vamps on, Hirsch changing the page for him. The minute he regards the next lyrics he innovates some slight hints of the preceding creations as he morphs into very relaxed, cocktail-lounge sophistication for the piano stylings where people in restaurants usually converse without listening to the music. And, over this, Hirsch announces that Millie is next to be feted. The rhythm slows to accommodate a ballad, the kind where the piano-player is dreaming of love with a perfect person. The lyrics require a Noel Coward-y touch at the keyboard as Stone tries to emulate the playwright's love of self-parody. He lightly delivers Millie's words and his tune:

"Ah……music……to let your eyes think in secret

while the brain dreamzzz

My life is doubly

'cause I hang around the bubbly."

Slut and hellcat
witch and hag

too much makeup
Fascist bag!"

Big finish as last line repeated. Everybody joins in.

"Now we finish with much more lyric from much more of a man," says Stone, softly taking over from Hirsch. "Father Fabulous! But give me a drink first." Host pours him one and takes it over to him. "I Love to drink!" he announces slowly and loudly. "No, man! That's Pather P's title!" says the hipster and out comes:

"You never would believe it but I have been
to fifteen parties tonight.

<a comical, boozy vocal now presents itself>

I've had whiskey sours and cocktails with gin
So excuse me if I'm just a bit im　　po　　lite!

I love to drink!

I like to take a bonded bottle
and with just a little shot, I'll
find a cozy little spot to go kerplunk in.

"I love to drink!

I don't want no one 'round to mess up
or I'll send an SOS up
for a suit to really dress up
and get drunk in.

The calendar has its holidays, no reason to stay
sober.
Birthdays, wars, July Fours, and Halloweens in
October.

"I love to drink.

The Klu Klux Klan, they never sinned
until their garments they unpinned
and they got three sheets to the wind.
I love to drink,

Now there are those who never drink, and of
them I will say:
when they wake up in the morning,
that's as good as you're gonna feel all day.

"I love to drink.

pink elephants go on a spree,
And I will gladly guarantee
When they get drunk, why, they see me.
I love to drink,

I had a friend, they called him Sydney,
Drank so much he ruined a kidney
But he had a good time didn' heeeeeeee?

'cause   I-I-I-I-I-I-I-I   luv   to   drrrrrrrrrink!"

**Shouts of '*bravo*' and vigorous applause and
some go over to shake the priest's hand. Freeman
and I stand together and keep clapping even as**

the others are expressing their delight and then to the piano to congratulate the composer.

"That was absolutely great!" shouts Freeman. "How did you do it"

"Like, who knows?" is the response. "I never got this far before."

I say, "Well, you spent all night on it, man."

A big smile comes out of him. "Playin' the piano is like being drunk. It's you plus someone else."

"Jeezus!" side-mouths Freeman.

XLIV

Host brings out a tape machine. "You must do that one again, you bloke. Into the recorder."

The Man starts right in playing and singing, and I need the loo. All are swarmed about the piano as I leave their company for the little boys', the six together in private euphoria and now their chattering muffled down beyond the door. Meantime, lordy, I have to go, and one always seems to have the most urgency whenever his system realizes it is very near the toidy. Yeah. There it is. Oh brother. Ahhh. At last. Now to the sink and the ever-perfidious mirror. What is that face saying? Is writing self-poisoning? We throw a variety of fictional characters at the reader. While we are actually populating the world with ghosts, the remains of those personages who won't depart the readers' memory. What is the ideal anyway? Calvino wrote that a classic is a book which even when we read it for the first time, gives the sense of rereading something perused before. The present, however, belongs to me. My six are out there in alphabetical disorder. Just as I wanted.

"I won't have the guts to fight you," the priest is saying when I re-enter the room. But saying it to whom? My God, it's Doll. These two?! No.

A smile comes out of Doll as she takes Father's arm. "Come, your grace. It's me for you. I'd even give you a kiss but I've just done my hair. It's easy to see you are the perfect man, sir. I will learn good deeds. *Mitzvahs*, right, Millie? And, and!" All her fascination is trained on the parson. "Here's a man after my own heart instead of everything else. Can't you see it?" The priest is too fascinated to be baffled and obviously not up to but quite willing for her appeal and her charming interest. "I even know one Latin phrase for you," she gushes. "Keep up with me now." Closes her eyes: "*Circa trova.*"

"Good gracious heavens. '*Seek and ye shall find.*' How very wonderful. We'll just go with the feeling, what do you say?" he effuses.

"Maybe we'll get to seek and to find out how sexually oriented you actually arrrr, Father. No! I don't mean that. I really don't because, at last, a man I can enjoy who won't just be another heat-seeking missile."

I look at Freeman standing next to me. He leans over to whisper. "He's a miniskirt away from being gay as a goose."

"Stop thinking like a tourist!" I answer him in low-voice kind.

He suddenly sees Millie absolutely beaming at him.

And now, it's STONE. Stone, all gangly and golly-whiz, holding hands with Hirsch. These two together are the real maverick-fit of them all. He's saying, "….and I finally have a frail who's not just another chick in a necklace of tears. She digs my shit and she's down with me doing lots more tunes."

"My talent consists of leaping into the fire so here I go again," she chortles.

Millie stands up and looks all around just like a bird does. Now she methodically counts the heads, pointing a finger at each person and mouthing the numbers. She finishes. "Well, Mr. Freeman, it seems we are the only ones unspoken for. I know you won't run out of laughs and I won't run out of legal currency. Good combination, *n'est-ce pas*?"

"Thank you so so much," gushes Freeman. "Have I found a new world where, at last, I can become the rich sleeper?" he asks plaintively.

"If you can't be kind, at least be vague," she tells him.

"All right. We'll split the car insurance," says he.

And my line to everyone: "I'm in the bathroom five minutes, and it's daffodils and match-ups all over the place," even though no one seems to be listening.

"Well, Sir Host," Father is saying, "you have danced your ambiguities and mysteries across our senses, and we are surely successfully vaccinated for writers' addiction. Thanks to your guidance, I have come to realize that being an author is being in jail. You are convicted of your crime the minute you begin your novel or your article or your poem or your love letter and you serve your sentence until the work is complete if we can forgive the *double-entendre*. I therefore announce that I am cured of my scripturgia and, instead, I will have a Doll to play with and to be my companion which is what dolls are created for."

"Will any of you ever write again?" Hirsch wonders.

Doll is beaming with delight. "Can someone find a phone. We all need transportation."

"Let's take a ride to Key West for some jammin'." proposes Stone.

"Wrong end of the bridge!" cites Doll.

Host announces he has already ordered taxicabs.

The doorbell rings, Stone plays a chord to fit its note: B-flat, D, F-sharp and A.

"Let it ring," says Millie. "It's probably the butler."

The entrance-way is opened to a flood of sunshine. The six step outside and then, as if answering their curtain call, turn back to Host.

The priest bows. "Literature! Literature indeed! This was life, this was passion."

"I realize I've always had freedom," announces Hirsch. "But it just felt like loneliness. I'm through chasing love now I've got jazz." She does a few, quick jitterbug steps with Stone.

"The last thing I ever wanted to do was hurt you," says Freeman.

"It's probably still on the list," she quips. They both laugh. Everyone walks to a waiting minivan, each pausing to wave goodbye and shout thank-you's. I hear Freeman telling the cabbie, "To the next festival, please!"

I follow along wondering what I will do. "Wait for me," I shout at the characters. But the presence of the separate conveyance means the author in search is soon to be the writer insouciant, as my sextet figuratively follow John Muir's "Throw a loaf a bread into an old sack and jump over the back fence."

Thus it is that all characters, real or imagined, exist to be understood or, at least, loved.

And will my creativity transcend desperate interest in approval now? Shouldn't I give up my temporary scripturgia and vow to donate everything I might make on book sales? What a thrill then just to launch a brand new Charity Foundation and all income for the poor and needy!

Oh, oh, oh. I am almost forgetting Host's gift of Carlos Primero. As I step back into the dwelling, I observe the man seated with his back to me as he taps a few words into his kitchen laptop.

"Shall we ever meet again," he asks without turning around.

"I don't know, dear friend. You found ME!" I say to him.

And I cannot resist sneaking a look over his shoulder. He has written:

a (very) forward

FOREWARD

by Grim Reader